C-2966   CAREER EXAMINATION SERIES

This is your
PASSBOOK for...

Accountant I

Test Preparation Study Guide
Questions & Answers

COPYRIGHT NOTICE

This book is SOLELY intended for, is sold ONLY to, and its use is RESTRICTED to individual, bona fide applicants or candidates who qualify by virtue of having seriously filed applications for appropriate license, certificate, professional and/or promotional advancement, higher school matriculation, scholarship, or other legitimate requirements of education and/or governmental authorities.

This book is NOT intended for use, class instruction, tutoring, training, duplication, copying, reprinting, excerption, or adaptation, etc., by:

1) Other publishers
2) Proprietors and/or Instructors of "Coaching" and/or Preparatory Courses
3) Personnel and/or Training Divisions of commercial, industrial, and governmental organizations
4) Schools, colleges, or universities and/or their departments and staffs, including teachers and other personnel
5) Testing Agencies or Bureaus
6) Study groups which seek by the purchase of a single volume to copy and/or duplicate and/or adapt this material for use by the group as a whole without having purchased individual volumes for each of the members of the group
7) Et al.

Such persons would be in violation of appropriate Federal and State statutes.

PROVISION OF LICENSING AGREEMENTS – Recognized educational, commercial, industrial, and governmental institutions and organizations, and others legitimately engaged in educational pursuits, including training, testing, and measurement activities, may address request for a licensing agreement to the copyright owners, who will determine whether, and under what conditions, including fees and charges, the materials in this book may be used them. In other words, a licensing facility exists for the legitimate use of the material in this book on other than an individual basis. However, it is asseverated and affirmed here that the material in this book CANNOT be used without the receipt of the express permission of such a licensing agreement from the Publishers. Inquiries re licensing should be addressed to the company, attention rights and permissions department.

All rights reserved, including the right of reproduction in whole or in part, in any form or by any means, electronic or mechanical, including photocopying, recording, or by any information storage and retrieval system, without permission in writing from the Publisher.

Copyright © 2024 by
National Learning Corporation

212 Michael Drive, Syosset, NY 11791
(516) 921-8888 • www.passbooks.com
E-mail: info@passbooks.com

PUBLISHED IN THE UNITED STATES OF AMERICA

PASSBOOK® SERIES

THE *PASSBOOK® SERIES* has been created to prepare applicants and candidates for the ultimate academic battlefield – the examination room.

At some time in our lives, each and every one of us may be required to take an examination – for validation, matriculation, admission, qualification, registration, certification, or licensure.

Based on the assumption that every applicant or candidate has met the basic formal educational standards, has taken the required number of courses, and read the necessary texts, the *PASSBOOK® SERIES* furnishes the one special preparation which may assure passing with confidence, instead of failing with insecurity. Examination questions – together with answers – are furnished as the basic vehicle for study so that the mysteries of the examination and its compounding difficulties may be eliminated or diminished by a sure method.

This book is meant to help you pass your examination provided that you qualify and are serious in your objective.

The entire field is reviewed through the huge store of content information which is succinctly presented through a provocative and challenging approach – the question-and-answer method.

A climate of success is established by furnishing the correct answers at the end of each test.

You soon learn to recognize types of questions, forms of questions, and patterns of questioning. You may even begin to anticipate expected outcomes.

You perceive that many questions are repeated or adapted so that you can gain acute insights, which may enable you to score many sure points.

You learn how to confront new questions, or types of questions, and to attack them confidently and work out the correct answers.

You note objectives and emphases, and recognize pitfalls and dangers, so that you may make positive educational adjustments.

Moreover, you are kept fully informed in relation to new concepts, methods, practices, and directions in the field.

You discover that you are actually taking the examination all the time: you are preparing for the examination by "taking" an examination, not by reading extraneous and/or supererogatory textbooks.

In short, this PASSBOOK®, used directedly, should be an important factor in helping you to pass your test.

ACCOUNTANT I

DUTIES
   Performs professional accounting work in accordance with established procedures and regulations; performs related duties as required.

NATURE OF WORK:
   This is professional accounting work in the classification, analysis and reporting of financial data. Employees of this class analyze financial transactions and prepare financial statements and reports to control and account for county funds and to analyze and project financial data. Work involves the application of governmental accounting principles and techniques to the treatment of transactions and other accounting operations. Supervision may be exercised over technical and clerical assistants. Work is performed within the framework of established policies and procedures, under the direction of a professional superior who provides advice and occasionally checks work in progress or upon completion. Performance also is evaluated through internal control systems.

ILLUSTRATIVE TASKS:
   Maintains and supervises the maintenance of accounting records; conducts standard internal audits of various county revenues and funds and departmental accounting records; ascertains that the distribution of all general journal entries are reasonable and correct; performs special audits as assigned.
   Maintains and analyzes fiscal records, audits, and evaluates all receipts; maintains and evaluates all expenditure forms, purchase orders and disbursement orders for compliance with established regulations and policies.
   May supervise the posting of accounting data to general ledger accounts from accounting records and documents; makes general journal entries as required; takes balances and prepares financial reports and statements.
   Analyzes accounting records and reports and prepares special management budget reports as requested.

KNOWLEDGE, ABILITIES AND SKILLS
- Knowledge of governmental accounting principles and practices.
- Knowledge of a variety of standard accounting and office procedures and equipment, including the application of electronic data processing to the maintenance and analysis of fiscal data.
- Ability to apply accounting principles and practices to the maintenance and analysis of fiscal and accounting records.

SUBJECT OF EXAMINATION:
The written test is designed to test for knowledge, skills, and/or abilities in such areas as:
1. General accounting and auditing;
2. Understanding and interpreting tabular material;
3. Understanding and interpreting written material; and
4. Preparing written material.

HOW TO TAKE A TEST

I. YOU MUST PASS AN EXAMINATION

A. WHAT EVERY CANDIDATE SHOULD KNOW

Examination applicants often ask us for help in preparing for the written test. What can I study in advance? What kinds of questions will be asked? How will the test be given? How will the papers be graded?

As an applicant for a civil service examination, you may be wondering about some of these things. Our purpose here is to suggest effective methods of advance study and to describe civil service examinations.

Your chances for success on this examination can be increased if you know how to prepare. Those "pre-examination jitters" can be reduced if you know what to expect. You can even experience an adventure in good citizenship if you know why civil service exams are given.

B. WHY ARE CIVIL SERVICE EXAMINATIONS GIVEN?

Civil service examinations are important to you in two ways. As a citizen, you want public jobs filled by employees who know how to do their work. As a job seeker, you want a fair chance to compete for that job on an equal footing with other candidates. The best-known means of accomplishing this two-fold goal is the competitive examination.

Exams are widely publicized throughout the nation. They may be administered for jobs in federal, state, city, municipal, town or village governments or agencies.

Any citizen may apply, with some limitations, such as the age or residence of applicants. Your experience and education may be reviewed to see whether you meet the requirements for the particular examination. When these requirements exist, they are reasonable and applied consistently to all applicants. Thus, a competitive examination may cause you some uneasiness now, but it is your privilege and safeguard.

C. HOW ARE CIVIL SERVICE EXAMS DEVELOPED?

Examinations are carefully written by trained technicians who are specialists in the field known as "psychological measurement," in consultation with recognized authorities in the field of work that the test will cover. These experts recommend the subject matter areas or skills to be tested; only those knowledges or skills important to your success on the job are included. The most reliable books and source materials available are used as references. Together, the experts and technicians judge the difficulty level of the questions.

Test technicians know how to phrase questions so that the problem is clearly stated. Their ethics do not permit "trick" or "catch" questions. Questions may have been tried out on sample groups, or subjected to statistical analysis, to determine their usefulness.

Written tests are often used in combination with performance tests, ratings of training and experience, and oral interviews. All of these measures combine to form the best-known means of finding the right person for the right job.

II. HOW TO PASS THE WRITTEN TEST

A. NATURE OF THE EXAMINATION

To prepare intelligently for civil service examinations, you should know how they differ from school examinations you have taken. In school you were assigned certain definite pages to read or subjects to cover. The examination questions were quite detailed and usually emphasized memory. Civil service exams, on the other hand, try to discover your present ability to perform the duties of a position, plus your potentiality to learn these duties. In other words, a civil service exam attempts to predict how successful you will be. Questions cover such a broad area that they cannot be as minute and detailed as school exam questions.

In the public service similar kinds of work, or positions, are grouped together in one "class." This process is known as *position-classification*. All the positions in a class are paid according to the salary range for that class. One class title covers all of these positions, and they are all tested by the same examination.

B. FOUR BASIC STEPS

1) Study the announcement

How, then, can you know what subjects to study? Our best answer is: "Learn as much as possible about the class of positions for which you've applied." The exam will test the knowledge, skills and abilities needed to do the work.

Your most valuable source of information about the position you want is the official exam announcement. This announcement lists the training and experience qualifications. Check these standards and apply only if you come reasonably close to meeting them.

The brief description of the position in the examination announcement offers some clues to the subjects which will be tested. Think about the job itself. Review the duties in your mind. Can you perform them, or are there some in which you are rusty? Fill in the blank spots in your preparation.

Many jurisdictions preview the written test in the exam announcement by including a section called "Knowledge and Abilities Required," "Scope of the Examination," or some similar heading. Here you will find out specifically what fields will be tested.

2) Review your own background

Once you learn in general what the position is all about, and what you need to know to do the work, ask yourself which subjects you already know fairly well and which need improvement. You may wonder whether to concentrate on improving your strong areas or on building some background in your fields of weakness. When the announcement has specified "some knowledge" or "considerable knowledge," or has used adjectives like "beginning principles of..." or "advanced ... methods," you can get a clue as to the number and difficulty of questions to be asked in any given field. More questions, and hence broader coverage, would be included for those subjects which are more important in the work. Now weigh your strengths and weaknesses against the job requirements and prepare accordingly.

3) Determine the level of the position

Another way to tell how intensively you should prepare is to understand the level of the job for which you are applying. Is it the entering level? In other words, is this the position in which beginners in a field of work are hired? Or is it an intermediate or advanced level? Sometimes this is indicated by such words as "Junior" or "Senior" in the class title. Other jurisdictions use Roman numerals to designate the level – Clerk I, Clerk II, for example. The word "Supervisor" sometimes appears in the title. If the level is not indicated by the title, check the description of duties. Will you be working under very close supervision, or will you have responsibility for independent decisions in this work?

4) Choose appropriate study materials

Now that you know the subjects to be examined and the relative amount of each subject to be covered, you can choose suitable study materials. For beginning level jobs, or even advanced ones, if you have a pronounced weakness in some aspect of your training, read a modern, standard textbook in that field. Be sure it is up to date and has general coverage. Such books are normally available at your library, and the librarian will be glad to help you locate one. For entry-level positions, questions of appropriate difficulty are chosen -- neither highly advanced questions, nor those too simple. Such questions require careful thought but not advanced training.

If the position for which you are applying is technical or advanced, you will read more advanced, specialized material. If you are already familiar with the basic principles of your field, elementary textbooks would waste your time. Concentrate on advanced textbooks and technical periodicals. Think through the concepts and review difficult problems in your field.

These are all general sources. You can get more ideas on your own initiative, following these leads. For example, training manuals and publications of the government agency which employs workers in your field can be useful, particularly for technical and professional positions. A letter or visit to the government department involved may result in more specific study suggestions, and certainly will provide you with a more definite idea of the exact nature of the position you are seeking.

III. KINDS OF TESTS

Tests are used for purposes other than measuring knowledge and ability to perform specified duties. For some positions, it is equally important to test ability to make adjustments to new situations or to profit from training. In others, basic mental abilities not dependent on information are essential. Questions which test these things may not appear as pertinent to the duties of the position as those which test for knowledge and information. Yet they are often highly important parts of a fair examination. For very general questions, it is almost impossible to help you direct your study efforts. What we can do is to point out some of the more common of these general abilities needed in public service positions and describe some typical questions.

1) General information

Broad, general information has been found useful for predicting job success in some kinds of work. This is tested in a variety of ways, from vocabulary lists to questions about current events. Basic background in some field of work, such as sociology or economics, may be sampled in a group of questions. Often these are principles which have become familiar to most persons through exposure rather than through formal training. It is difficult to advise you how to study for these questions; being alert to the world around you is our best suggestion.

2) Verbal ability

An example of an ability needed in many positions is verbal or language ability. Verbal ability is, in brief, the ability to use and understand words. Vocabulary and grammar tests are typical measures of this ability. Reading comprehension or paragraph interpretation questions are common in many kinds of civil service tests. You are given a paragraph of written material and asked to find its central meaning.

3) Numerical ability

Number skills can be tested by the familiar arithmetic problem, by checking paired lists of numbers to see which are alike and which are different, or by interpreting charts and graphs. In the latter test, a graph may be printed in the test booklet which you are asked to use as the basis for answering questions.

4) Observation

A popular test for law-enforcement positions is the observation test. A picture is shown to you for several minutes, then taken away. Questions about the picture test your ability to observe both details and larger elements.

5) Following directions

In many positions in the public service, the employee must be able to carry out written instructions dependably and accurately. You may be given a chart with several columns, each column listing a variety of information. The questions require you to carry out directions involving the information given in the chart.

6) Skills and aptitudes

Performance tests effectively measure some manual skills and aptitudes. When the skill is one in which you are trained, such as typing or shorthand, you can practice. These tests are often very much like those given in business school or high school courses. For many of the other skills and aptitudes, however, no short-time preparation can be made. Skills and abilities natural to you or that you have developed throughout your lifetime are being tested.

Many of the general questions just described provide all the data needed to answer the questions and ask you to use your reasoning ability to find the answers. Your best preparation for these tests, as well as for tests of facts and ideas, is to be at your physical and mental best. You, no doubt, have your own methods of getting into an exam-taking mood and keeping "in shape." The next section lists some ideas on this subject.

IV. KINDS OF QUESTIONS

Only rarely is the "essay" question, which you answer in narrative form, used in civil service tests. Civil service tests are usually of the short-answer type. Full instructions for answering these questions will be given to you at the examination. But in case this is your first experience with short-answer questions and separate answer sheets, here is what you need to know:

1) Multiple-choice Questions

Most popular of the short-answer questions is the "multiple choice" or "best answer" question. It can be used, for example, to test for factual knowledge, ability to solve problems or judgment in meeting situations found at work.

A multiple-choice question is normally one of three types—
- It can begin with an incomplete statement followed by several possible endings. You are to find the one ending which *best* completes the statement, although some of the others may not be entirely wrong.
- It can also be a complete statement in the form of a question which is answered by choosing one of the statements listed.

- It can be in the form of a problem – again you select the best answer.

Here is an example of a multiple-choice question with a discussion which should give you some clues as to the method for choosing the right answer:

When an employee has a complaint about his assignment, the action which will *best* help him overcome his difficulty is to
- A. discuss his difficulty with his coworkers
- B. take the problem to the head of the organization
- C. take the problem to the person who gave him the assignment
- D. say nothing to anyone about his complaint

In answering this question, you should study each of the choices to find which is best. Consider choice "A" – Certainly an employee may discuss his complaint with fellow employees, but no change or improvement can result, and the complaint remains unresolved. Choice "B" is a poor choice since the head of the organization probably does not know what assignment you have been given, and taking your problem to him is known as "going over the head" of the supervisor. The supervisor, or person who made the assignment, is the person who can clarify it or correct any injustice. Choice "C" is, therefore, correct. To say nothing, as in choice "D," is unwise. Supervisors have and interest in knowing the problems employees are facing, and the employee is seeking a solution to his problem.

2) True/False Questions

The "true/false" or "right/wrong" form of question is sometimes used. Here a complete statement is given. Your job is to decide whether the statement is right or wrong.

SAMPLE: A roaming cell-phone call to a nearby city costs less than a non-roaming call to a distant city.

This statement is wrong, or false, since roaming calls are more expensive.

This is not a complete list of all possible question forms, although most of the others are variations of these common types. You will always get complete directions for answering questions. Be sure you understand *how* to mark your answers – ask questions until you do.

V. RECORDING YOUR ANSWERS

Computer terminals are used more and more today for many different kinds of exams.
For an examination with very few applicants, you may be told to record your answers in the test booklet itself. Separate answer sheets are much more common. If this separate answer sheet is to be scored by machine – and this is often the case – it is highly important that you mark your answers correctly in order to get credit.
An electronic scoring machine is often used in civil service offices because of the speed with which papers can be scored. Machine-scored answer sheets must be marked with a pencil, which will be given to you. This pencil has a high graphite content which responds to the electronic scoring machine. As a matter of fact, stray dots may register as answers, so do not let your pencil rest on the answer sheet while you are pondering the correct answer. Also, if your pencil lead breaks or is otherwise defective, ask for another.

Since the answer sheet will be dropped in a slot in the scoring machine, be careful not to bend the corners or get the paper crumpled.

The answer sheet normally has five vertical columns of numbers, with 30 numbers to a column. These numbers correspond to the question numbers in your test booklet. After each number, going across the page are four or five pairs of dotted lines. These short dotted lines have small letters or numbers above them. The first two pairs may also have a "T" or "F" above the letters. This indicates that the first two pairs only are to be used if the questions are of the true-false type. If the questions are multiple choice, disregard the "T" and "F" and pay attention only to the small letters or numbers.

Answer your questions in the manner of the sample that follows:

32. The largest city in the United States is
    A. Washington, D.C.
    B. New York City
    C. Chicago
    D. Detroit
    E. San Francisco

1) Choose the answer you think is best. (New York City is the largest, so "B" is correct.)
2) Find the row of dotted lines numbered the same as the question you are answering. (Find row number 32)
3) Find the pair of dotted lines corresponding to the answer. (Find the pair of lines under the mark "B.")
4) Make a solid black mark between the dotted lines.

VI. BEFORE THE TEST

Common sense will help you find procedures to follow to get ready for an examination. Too many of us, however, overlook these sensible measures. Indeed, nervousness and fatigue have been found to be the most serious reasons why applicants fail to do their best on civil service tests. Here is a list of reminders:

- Begin your preparation early – Don't wait until the last minute to go scurrying around for books and materials or to find out what the position is all about.
- Prepare continuously – An hour a night for a week is better than an all-night cram session. This has been definitely established. What is more, a night a week for a month will return better dividends than crowding your study into a shorter period of time.
- Locate the place of the exam – You have been sent a notice telling you when and where to report for the examination. If the location is in a different town or otherwise unfamiliar to you, it would be well to inquire the best route and learn something about the building.
- Relax the night before the test – Allow your mind to rest. Do not study at all that night. Plan some mild recreation or diversion; then go to bed early and get a good night's sleep.
- Get up early enough to make a leisurely trip to the place for the test – This way unforeseen events, traffic snarls, unfamiliar buildings, etc. will not upset you.
- Dress comfortably – A written test is not a fashion show. You will be known by number and not by name, so wear something comfortable.

- Leave excess paraphernalia at home – Shopping bags and odd bundles will get in your way. You need bring only the items mentioned in the official notice you received; usually everything you need is provided. Do not bring reference books to the exam. They will only confuse those last minutes and be taken away from you when in the test room.
- Arrive somewhat ahead of time – If because of transportation schedules you must get there very early, bring a newspaper or magazine to take your mind off yourself while waiting.
- Locate the examination room – When you have found the proper room, you will be directed to the seat or part of the room where you will sit. Sometimes you are given a sheet of instructions to read while you are waiting. Do not fill out any forms until you are told to do so; just read them and be prepared.
- Relax and prepare to listen to the instructions
- If you have any physical problem that may keep you from doing your best, be sure to tell the test administrator. If you are sick or in poor health, you really cannot do your best on the exam. You can come back and take the test some other time.

VII. AT THE TEST

The day of the test is here and you have the test booklet in your hand. The temptation to get going is very strong. Caution! There is more to success than knowing the right answers. You must know how to identify your papers and understand variations in the type of short-answer question used in this particular examination. Follow these suggestions for maximum results from your efforts:

1) Cooperate with the monitor

The test administrator has a duty to create a situation in which you can be as much at ease as possible. He will give instructions, tell you when to begin, check to see that you are marking your answer sheet correctly, and so on. He is not there to guard you, although he will see that your competitors do not take unfair advantage. He wants to help you do your best.

2) Listen to all instructions

Don't jump the gun! Wait until you understand all directions. In most civil service tests you get more time than you need to answer the questions. So don't be in a hurry. Read each word of instructions until you clearly understand the meaning. Study the examples, listen to all announcements and follow directions. Ask questions if you do not understand what to do.

3) Identify your papers

Civil service exams are usually identified by number only. You will be assigned a number; you must not put your name on your test papers. Be sure to copy your number correctly. Since more than one exam may be given, copy your exact examination title.

4) Plan your time

Unless you are told that a test is a "speed" or "rate of work" test, speed itself is usually not important. Time enough to answer all the questions will be provided, but this does not mean that you have all day. An overall time limit has been set. Divide the total time (in minutes) by the number of questions to determine the approximate time you have for each question.

5) Do not linger over difficult questions

If you come across a difficult question, mark it with a paper clip (useful to have along) and come back to it when you have been through the booklet. One caution if you do this – be sure to skip a number on your answer sheet as well. Check often to be sure that you have not lost your place and that you are marking in the row numbered the same as the question you are answering.

6) Read the questions

Be sure you know what the question asks! Many capable people are unsuccessful because they failed to *read* the questions correctly.

7) Answer all questions

Unless you have been instructed that a penalty will be deducted for incorrect answers, it is better to guess than to omit a question.

8) Speed tests

It is often better NOT to guess on speed tests. It has been found that on timed tests people are tempted to spend the last few seconds before time is called in marking answers at random – without even reading them – in the hope of picking up a few extra points. To discourage this practice, the instructions may warn you that your score will be "corrected" for guessing. That is, a penalty will be applied. The incorrect answers will be deducted from the correct ones, or some other penalty formula will be used.

9) Review your answers

If you finish before time is called, go back to the questions you guessed or omitted to give them further thought. Review other answers if you have time.

10) Return your test materials

If you are ready to leave before others have finished or time is called, take ALL your materials to the monitor and leave quietly. Never take any test material with you. The monitor can discover whose papers are not complete, and taking a test booklet may be grounds for disqualification.

VIII. EXAMINATION TECHNIQUES

1) Read the general instructions carefully. These are usually printed on the first page of the exam booklet. As a rule, these instructions refer to the timing of the examination; the fact that you should not start work until the signal and must stop work at a signal, etc. If there are any *special* instructions, such as a choice of questions to be answered, make sure that you note this instruction carefully.

2) When you are ready to start work on the examination, that is as soon as the signal has been given, read the instructions to each question booklet, underline any key words or phrases, such as *least, best, outline, describe* and the like. In this way you will tend to answer as requested rather than discover on reviewing your paper that you *listed without describing*, that you selected the *worst* choice rather than the *best* choice, etc.

3) If the examination is of the objective or multiple-choice type – that is, each question will also give a series of possible answers: A, B, C or D, and you are called upon to select the best answer and write the letter next to that answer on your answer paper – it is advisable to start answering each question in turn. There may be anywhere from 50 to 100 such questions in the three or four hours allotted and you can see how much time would be taken if you read through all the questions before beginning to answer any. Furthermore, if you come across a question or group of questions which you know would be difficult to answer, it would undoubtedly affect your handling of all the other questions.

4) If the examination is of the essay type and contains but a few questions, it is a moot point as to whether you should read all the questions before starting to answer any one. Of course, if you are given a choice – say five out of seven and the like – then it is essential to read all the questions so you can eliminate the two that are most difficult. If, however, you are asked to answer all the questions, there may be danger in trying to answer the easiest one first because you may find that you will spend too much time on it. The best technique is to answer the first question, then proceed to the second, etc.

5) Time your answers. Before the exam begins, write down the time it started, then add the time allowed for the examination and write down the time it must be completed, then divide the time available somewhat as follows:
   - If 3-1/2 hours are allowed, that would be 210 minutes. If you have 80 objective-type questions, that would be an average of 2-1/2 minutes per question. Allow yourself no more than 2 minutes per question, or a total of 160 minutes, which will permit about 50 minutes to review.
   - If for the time allotment of 210 minutes there are 7 essay questions to answer, that would average about 30 minutes a question. Give yourself only 25 minutes per question so that you have about 35 minutes to review.

6) The most important instruction is to *read each question* and make sure you know what is wanted. The second most important instruction is to *time yourself properly* so that you answer every question. The third most important instruction is to *answer every question*. Guess if you have to but include something for each question. Remember that you will receive no credit for a blank and will probably receive some credit if you write something in answer to an essay question. If you guess a letter – say "B" for a multiple-choice question – you may have guessed right. If you leave a blank as an answer to a multiple-choice question, the examiners may respect your feelings but it will not add a point to your score. Some exams may penalize you for wrong answers, so in such cases *only*, you may not want to guess unless you have some basis for your answer.

7) Suggestions
   a. Objective-type questions
      1. Examine the question booklet for proper sequence of pages and questions
      2. Read all instructions carefully
      3. Skip any question which seems too difficult; return to it after all other questions have been answered
      4. Apportion your time properly; do not spend too much time on any single question or group of questions

5. Note and underline key words – *all, most, fewest, least, best, worst, same, opposite,* etc.
6. Pay particular attention to negatives
7. Note unusual option, e.g., unduly long, short, complex, different or similar in content to the body of the question
8. Observe the use of "hedging" words – *probably, may, most likely,* etc.
9. Make sure that your answer is put next to the same number as the question
10. Do not second-guess unless you have good reason to believe the second answer is definitely more correct
11. Cross out original answer if you decide another answer is more accurate; do not erase until you are ready to hand your paper in
12. Answer all questions; guess unless instructed otherwise
13. Leave time for review

   b. Essay questions
      1. Read each question carefully
      2. Determine exactly what is wanted. Underline key words or phrases.
      3. Decide on outline or paragraph answer
      4. Include many different points and elements unless asked to develop any one or two points or elements
      5. Show impartiality by giving pros and cons unless directed to select one side only
      6. Make and write down any assumptions you find necessary to answer the questions
      7. Watch your English, grammar, punctuation and choice of words
      8. Time your answers; don't crowd material

8) Answering the essay question

Most essay questions can be answered by framing the specific response around several key words or ideas. Here are a few such key words or ideas:

M's: manpower, materials, methods, money, management
P's: purpose, program, policy, plan, procedure, practice, problems, pitfalls, personnel, public relations

   a. Six basic steps in handling problems:
      1. Preliminary plan and background development
      2. Collect information, data and facts
      3. Analyze and interpret information, data and facts
      4. Analyze and develop solutions as well as make recommendations
      5. Prepare report and sell recommendations
      6. Install recommendations and follow up effectiveness

   b. Pitfalls to avoid
      1. *Taking things for granted* – A statement of the situation does not necessarily imply that each of the elements is necessarily true; for example, a complaint may be invalid and biased so that all that can be taken for granted is that a complaint has been registered

2. *Considering only one side of a situation* – Wherever possible, indicate several alternatives and then point out the reasons you selected the best one
3. *Failing to indicate follow up* – Whenever your answer indicates action on your part, make certain that you will take proper follow-up action to see how successful your recommendations, procedures or actions turn out to be
4. *Taking too long in answering any single question* – Remember to time your answers properly

IX. AFTER THE TEST

Scoring procedures differ in detail among civil service jurisdictions although the general principles are the same. Whether the papers are hand-scored or graded by machine we have described, they are nearly always graded by number. That is, the person who marks the paper knows only the number – never the name – of the applicant. Not until all the papers have been graded will they be matched with names. If other tests, such as training and experience or oral interview ratings have been given, scores will be combined. Different parts of the examination usually have different weights. For example, the written test might count 60 percent of the final grade, and a rating of training and experience 40 percent. In many jurisdictions, veterans will have a certain number of points added to their grades.

After the final grade has been determined, the names are placed in grade order and an eligible list is established. There are various methods for resolving ties between those who get the same final grade – probably the most common is to place first the name of the person whose application was received first. Job offers are made from the eligible list in the order the names appear on it. You will be notified of your grade and your rank as soon as all these computations have been made. This will be done as rapidly as possible.

People who are found to meet the requirements in the announcement are called "eligibles." Their names are put on a list of eligible candidates. An eligible's chances of getting a job depend on how high he stands on this list and how fast agencies are filling jobs from the list.

When a job is to be filled from a list of eligibles, the agency asks for the names of people on the list of eligibles for that job. When the civil service commission receives this request, it sends to the agency the names of the three people highest on this list. Or, if the job to be filled has specialized requirements, the office sends the agency the names of the top three persons who meet these requirements from the general list.

The appointing officer makes a choice from among the three people whose names were sent to him. If the selected person accepts the appointment, the names of the others are put back on the list to be considered for future openings.

That is the rule in hiring from all kinds of eligible lists, whether they are for typist, carpenter, chemist, or something else. For every vacancy, the appointing officer has his choice of any one of the top three eligibles on the list. This explains why the person whose name is on top of the list sometimes does not get an appointment when some of the persons lower on the list do. If the appointing officer chooses the second or third eligible, the No. 1 eligible does not get a job at once, but stays on the list until he is appointed or the list is terminated.

X. HOW TO PASS THE INTERVIEW TEST

The examination for which you applied requires an oral interview test. You have already taken the written test and you are now being called for the interview test – the final part of the formal examination.

You may think that it is not possible to prepare for an interview test and that there are no procedures to follow during an interview. Our purpose is to point out some things you can do in advance that will help you and some good rules to follow and pitfalls to avoid while you are being interviewed.

What is an interview supposed to test?

The written examination is designed to test the technical knowledge and competence of the candidate; the oral is designed to evaluate intangible qualities, not readily measured otherwise, and to establish a list showing the relative fitness of each candidate – as measured against his competitors – for the position sought. Scoring is not on the basis of "right" and "wrong," but on a sliding scale of values ranging from "not passable" to "outstanding." As a matter of fact, it is possible to achieve a relatively low score without a single "incorrect" answer because of evident weakness in the qualities being measured.

Occasionally, an examination may consist entirely of an oral test – either an individual or a group oral. In such cases, information is sought concerning the technical knowledges and abilities of the candidate, since there has been no written examination for this purpose. More commonly, however, an oral test is used to supplement a written examination.

Who conducts interviews?

The composition of oral boards varies among different jurisdictions. In nearly all, a representative of the personnel department serves as chairman. One of the members of the board may be a representative of the department in which the candidate would work. In some cases, "outside experts" are used, and, frequently, a businessman or some other representative of the general public is asked to serve. Labor and management or other special groups may be represented. The aim is to secure the services of experts in the appropriate field.

However the board is composed, it is a good idea (and not at all improper or unethical) to ascertain in advance of the interview who the members are and what groups they represent. When you are introduced to them, you will have some idea of their backgrounds and interests, and at least you will not stutter and stammer over their names.

What should be done before the interview?

While knowledge about the board members is useful and takes some of the surprise element out of the interview, there is other preparation which is more substantive. It *is* possible to prepare for an oral interview – in several ways:

1) Keep a copy of your application and review it carefully before the interview

This may be the only document before the oral board, and the starting point of the interview. Know what education and experience you have listed there, and the sequence and dates of all of it. Sometimes the board will ask you to review the highlights of your experience for them; you should not have to hem and haw doing it.

2) Study the class specification and the examination announcement

Usually, the oral board has one or both of these to guide them. The qualities, characteristics or knowledges required by the position sought are stated in these documents. They offer valuable clues as to the nature of the oral interview. For example, if the job involves supervisory responsibilities, the announcement will usually indicate that knowledge of modern supervisory methods and the qualifications of the candidate as a supervisor will be tested. If so, you can expect such questions, frequently in the form of a hypothetical situation which you are expected to solve. NEVER go into an oral without knowledge of the duties and responsibilities of the job you seek.

3) Think through each qualification required

Try to visualize the kind of questions you would ask if you were a board member. How well could you answer them? Try especially to appraise your own knowledge and background in each area, *measured against the job sought*, and identify any areas in which you are weak. Be critical and realistic – do not flatter yourself.

4) Do some general reading in areas in which you feel you may be weak

For example, if the job involves supervision and your past experience has NOT, some general reading in supervisory methods and practices, particularly in the field of human relations, might be useful. Do NOT study agency procedures or detailed manuals. The oral board will be testing your understanding and capacity, not your memory.

5) Get a good night's sleep and watch your general health and mental attitude

You will want a clear head at the interview. Take care of a cold or any other minor ailment, and of course, no hangovers.

What should be done on the day of the interview?

Now comes the day of the interview itself. Give yourself plenty of time to get there. Plan to arrive somewhat ahead of the scheduled time, particularly if your appointment is in the fore part of the day. If a previous candidate fails to appear, the board might be ready for you a bit early. By early afternoon an oral board is almost invariably behind schedule if there are many candidates, and you may have to wait. Take along a book or magazine to read, or your application to review, but leave any extraneous material in the waiting room when you go in for your interview. In any event, relax and compose yourself.

The matter of dress is important. The board is forming impressions about you – from your experience, your manners, your attitude, and your appearance. Give your personal appearance careful attention. Dress your best, but not your flashiest. Choose conservative, appropriate clothing, and be sure it is immaculate. This is a business interview, and your appearance should indicate that you regard it as such. Besides, being well groomed and properly dressed will help boost your confidence.

Sooner or later, someone will call your name and escort you into the interview room. *This is it.* From here on you are on your own. It is too late for any more preparation. But remember, you asked for this opportunity to prove your fitness, and you are here because your request was granted.

What happens when you go in?

The usual sequence of events will be as follows: The clerk (who is often the board stenographer) will introduce you to the chairman of the oral board, who will introduce you to the other members of the board. Acknowledge the introductions before you sit down. Do not be surprised if you find a microphone facing you or a stenotypist sitting by. Oral interviews are usually recorded in the event of an appeal or other review.

Usually the chairman of the board will open the interview by reviewing the highlights of your education and work experience from your application – primarily for the benefit of the other members of the board, as well as to get the material into the record. Do not interrupt or comment unless there is an error or significant misinterpretation; if that is the case, do not hesitate. But do not quibble about insignificant matters. Also, he will usually ask you some question about your education, experience or your present job – partly to get you to start talking and to establish the interviewing "rapport." He may start the actual questioning, or turn it over to one of the other members. Frequently, each member undertakes the questioning on a particular area, one in which he is perhaps most competent, so you can expect each member to participate in the examination. Because time is limited, you may also expect some rather abrupt switches in the direction the questioning takes, so do not be upset by it. Normally, a board member will not pursue a single line of questioning unless he discovers a particular strength or weakness.

After each member has participated, the chairman will usually ask whether any member has any further questions, then will ask you if you have anything you wish to add. Unless you are expecting this question, it may floor you. Worse, it may start you off on an extended, extemporaneous speech. The board is not usually seeking more information. The question is principally to offer you a last opportunity to present further qualifications or to indicate that you have nothing to add. So, if you feel that a significant qualification or characteristic has been overlooked, it is proper to point it out in a sentence or so. Do not compliment the board on the thoroughness of their examination – they have been sketchy, and you know it. If you wish, merely say, "No thank you, I have nothing further to add." This is a point where you can "talk yourself out" of a good impression or fail to present an important bit of information. Remember, *you close the interview yourself.*

The chairman will then say, "That is all, Mr. _____, thank you." Do not be startled; the interview is over, and quicker than you think. Thank him, gather your belongings and take your leave. Save your sigh of relief for the other side of the door.

How to put your best foot forward

Throughout this entire process, you may feel that the board individually and collectively is trying to pierce your defenses, seek out your hidden weaknesses and embarrass and confuse you. Actually, this is not true. They are obliged to make an appraisal of your qualifications for the job you are seeking, and they want to see you in your best light. Remember, they must interview all candidates and a non-cooperative candidate may become a failure in spite of their best efforts to bring out his qualifications. Here are 15 suggestions that will help you:

1) Be natural – Keep your attitude confident, not cocky

If you are not confident that you can do the job, do not expect the board to be. Do not apologize for your weaknesses, try to bring out your strong points. The board is interested in a positive, not negative, presentation. Cockiness will antagonize any board member and make him wonder if you are covering up a weakness by a false show of strength.

2) Get comfortable, but don't lounge or sprawl

Sit erectly but not stiffly. A careless posture may lead the board to conclude that you are careless in other things, or at least that you are not impressed by the importance of the occasion. Either conclusion is natural, even if incorrect. Do not fuss with your clothing, a pencil or an ashtray. Your hands may occasionally be useful to emphasize a point; do not let them become a point of distraction.

3) Do not wisecrack or make small talk

This is a serious situation, and your attitude should show that you consider it as such. Further, the time of the board is limited – they do not want to waste it, and neither should you.

4) Do not exaggerate your experience or abilities

In the first place, from information in the application or other interviews and sources, the board may know more about you than you think. Secondly, you probably will not get away with it. An experienced board is rather adept at spotting such a situation, so do not take the chance.

5) If you know a board member, do not make a point of it, yet do not hide it

Certainly you are not fooling him, and probably not the other members of the board. Do not try to take advantage of your acquaintanceship – it will probably do you little good.

6) Do not dominate the interview

Let the board do that. They will give you the clues – do not assume that you have to do all the talking. Realize that the board has a number of questions to ask you, and do not try to take up all the interview time by showing off your extensive knowledge of the answer to the first one.

7) Be attentive

You only have 20 minutes or so, and you should keep your attention at its sharpest throughout. When a member is addressing a problem or question to you, give him your undivided attention. Address your reply principally to him, but do not exclude the other board members.

8) Do not interrupt

A board member may be stating a problem for you to analyze. He will ask you a question when the time comes. Let him state the problem, and wait for the question.

9) Make sure you understand the question

Do not try to answer until you are sure what the question is. If it is not clear, restate it in your own words or ask the board member to clarify it for you. However, do not haggle about minor elements.

10) Reply promptly but not hastily

A common entry on oral board rating sheets is "candidate responded readily," or "candidate hesitated in replies." Respond as promptly and quickly as you can, but do not jump to a hasty, ill-considered answer.

11) Do not be peremptory in your answers

A brief answer is proper – but do not fire your answer back. That is a losing game from your point of view. The board member can probably ask questions much faster than you can answer them.

12) Do not try to create the answer you think the board member wants

He is interested in what kind of mind you have and how it works – not in playing games. Furthermore, he can usually spot this practice and will actually grade you down on it.

13) Do not switch sides in your reply merely to agree with a board member

Frequently, a member will take a contrary position merely to draw you out and to see if you are willing and able to defend your point of view. Do not start a debate, yet do not surrender a good position. If a position is worth taking, it is worth defending.

14) Do not be afraid to admit an error in judgment if you are shown to be wrong

The board knows that you are forced to reply without any opportunity for careful consideration. Your answer may be demonstrably wrong. If so, admit it and get on with the interview.

15) Do not dwell at length on your present job

The opening question may relate to your present assignment. Answer the question but do not go into an extended discussion. You are being examined for a *new* job, not your present one. As a matter of fact, try to phrase ALL your answers in terms of the job for which you are being examined.

Basis of Rating

Probably you will forget most of these "do's" and "don'ts" when you walk into the oral interview room. Even remembering them all will not ensure you a passing grade. Perhaps you did not have the qualifications in the first place. But remembering them will help you to put your best foot forward, without treading on the toes of the board members.

Rumor and popular opinion to the contrary notwithstanding, an oral board wants you to make the best appearance possible. They know you are under pressure – but they also want to see how you respond to it as a guide to what your reaction would be under the pressures of the job you seek. They will be influenced by the degree of poise you display, the personal traits you show and the manner in which you respond.

ABOUT THIS BOOK

This book contains tests divided into Examination Sections. Go through each test, answering every question in the margin. We have also attached a sample answer sheet at the back of the book that can be removed and used. At the end of each test look at the answer key and check your answers. On the ones you got wrong, look at the right answer choice and learn. Do not fill in the answers first. Do not memorize the questions and answers, but understand the answer and principles involved. On your test, the questions will likely be different from the samples. Questions are changed and new ones added. If you understand these past questions you should have success with any changes that arise. Tests may consist of several types of questions. We have additional books on each subject should more study be advisable or necessary for you. Finally, the more you study, the better prepared you will be. This book is intended to be the last thing you study before you walk into the examination room. Prior study of relevant texts is also recommended. NLC publishes some of these in our Fundamental Series. Knowledge and good sense are important factors in passing your exam. Good luck also helps. So now study this Passbook, absorb the material contained within and take that knowledge into the examination. Then do your best to pass that exam.

EXAMINATION SECTION

EXAMINATION SECTION
TEST 1

DIRECTIONS: Each question or incomplete statement is followed by several suggested answers or completions. Select the one that BEST answers the question or completes the statement. *PRINT THE LETTER OF THE CORRECT ANSWER IN THE SPACE AT THE RIGHT.*

1. The allowance for doubtful accounts represents the   1.____

   A. difference between the gross value of accounts receivable and the net realizable value of accounts receivable
   B. amount of uncollectible accounts written off to date
   C. difference between total credit sales and collection on credit sales
   D. cash set aside to compensate for bad debt losses

2. What is the term for the interest deducted from the face amount of a note payable?   2.____

   A. Discount
   B. Fee
   C. Levy
   D. Contingency

3. The Yardman purchases a mower from an equipment dealer on February 1 for $7,200. The dealer has guaranteed the mower to have a useful life of 10 years. Assuming adjusting entries are prepared monthly, the book value of the mower on June 30 is   3.____

   A. $300
   B. $6480
   C. $6900
   D. $7,200

4. Gullstart, Inc. had operating cash flows of $240,000, total cash flows of $1 million, and average total assets of $5 million. Its cash flow on total assets ratio is   4.____

   A. 3.6%
   B. 4.8%
   C. 5.0%
   D. 12.4%

5. Which of the following assets would NOT be depreciated?   5.____

   A. Buildings
   B. Servers/information systems
   C. Land
   D. Store fixtures

Questions 6-8 refer to the following information: On January 1, five years ago, Winkler and Dunnebier Machinery purchased an envelope machine for $1.5 million. The machine was given a useful life of 5 years or 40,000 hours. During the machine's 5-year life span, its hourly usage was, respectively, 4000; 8000; 16,000,; 10,000; and 2000 hours.

6. Using the double-declining balance method, calculate the depreciation expense for the FIRST year.

    A. $135,000
    B. $360,000
    C. $540,000
    D. $600,000

7. Using the units-of-production method, calculate the depreciation expense for the THIRD year.

    A. $129,600
    B. $216,000
    C. $337,500
    D. $540,000

8. Using the straight-line method, calculate the depreciation expense for the FIFTH year.

    A. $44,400
    B. $67,500
    C. $270,000
    D. $360,000

9. The _____ principle requires expenses to be reported in the same period as the revenues the were earned as a result of the expenses.

    A. realization
    B. cost
    C. matching
    D. going-concern

10. To recognize insurance expired during an accounting period, the adjusting entry will affect the _____ account.
    I. asset
    II. expense
    III. liability
    IV. revenue

    A. I and II
    B. II and III
    C. III and IV
    D. I, II, III and IV

11. Adjusting entries for annual financial statements are generally made

    A. at the beginning of the year
    B. after every transaction
    C. periodically throughout the year
    D. at the end of the year

12. In a ledger, debit entries

    A. decrease assets
    B. increase owners' equity

C. decrease liabilities
D. decrease profitability

13. What is the term for a person who signs a note receivable and promises to pay the principal and interest? 13._____

    A. Payee
    B. Holder
    C. Maker
    D. Recipient

14. Trusty, Inc. had net credit sales for the year of $120,000. Accounts receivable at year's end are $40,000, and there is a $200 credit in allowance for doubtful accounts. If Trusty estimates bad debt losses based on an aging of accounts receivable as $2400, the expense for the year is 14._____

    A. $200
    B. $2200
    C. $2400
    D. $2600

15. When bonds are issued at a discount, the discount 15._____

    A. appears on the balance sheet as a contra liability
    B. reduces the overall cost of borrowing
    C. appears on the income statement as other income
    D. appears on the income statement as an expense

16. Dividends become a liability on the date that 16._____

    A. the dividend is declared by the board of directors
    B. the dividend is recorded
    C. cumulative preferred stock dividends are declared in arrears
    D. payment of the dividends is made

17. The financial statement of a large corporation is MOST likely to include 17._____

    A. book value per share
    B. earnings per share
    C. the current ratio
    D. return on assets

18. _____ are long-term notes issued with a pledge of specified property, plant, and equipment for the loan. 18._____

    A. sinking-fund bonds
    B. mortgage notes payable
    C. bonds payable
    D. foreclosures

19. Empire Waste sold a truck that originally cost $200,000 for $120,000. The accumulated depreciation on the truck was $80,000. Empire Waste should record a

    A. $40,000 loss
    B. $40,000 gain
    C. $80,000 loss
    D. break-even transaction

20. The "chart of accounts" refers to a

    A. complete listing of the account titles to be used
    B. collection of all a company's accounts
    C. system of recording debit and credit entries for each transaction
    D. statement that shows the name and balance of all ledger accounts

21. If net credit sales for a given year are $800,000 and the average accounts receivable are $40,000, the accounts receivable turnover is

    A. 20
    B. 50
    C. 80
    D. 100

22. During a period of steadily rising prices, the _____ method of inventory valuation is likely to result in the lowest cost of goods sold.

    A. gross profit
    B. last in, first out (LIFO)
    C. first in, first out (FIFO)
    D. specific identification

23. On an income statement, each of the following would appear below income from continuing operations, EXCEPT

    A. discontinued operations
    B. net income
    C. extraordinary items
    D. cumulative effect of accounting changes related to previous years

24. During the month of December, the liabilities of Duckworth increased $26,000 and the owners' equity decreased $6000. The assets of Duckworth _____ during December.

    A. increased $20,000
    B. increased $22,000
    C. decreased $20,000
    D. decreased $32,000

25. At year's end, Lavender, Inc. is estimating its ending inventory. The following information is available:

Inventory as of October 1	$12,500
Net fourth-quarter sales	$40,000
Net fourth-quarter purchases	$27,500

Lavender typically achieves a gross profit of around 15%. Using the gross profit method, calculate Lavender's ending inventory.

A. $4000
B. $6000
C. $10,000
D. $16,000

KEY (CORRECT ANSWERS)

1. A
2. A
3. C
4. B
5. C

6. D
7. D
8. C
9. C
10. A

11. D
12. C
13. C
14. B
15. A

16. A
17. B
18. B
19. D
20. A

21. A
22. C
23. D
24. A
25. B

TEST 2

DIRECTIONS: Each question or incomplete statement is followed by several suggested answers or completions. Select the one that BEST answers the question or completes the statement. *PRINT THE LETTER OF THE CORRECT ANSWER IN THE SPACE AT THE RIGHT.*

1. Which of the following is a balance sheet item that represents the portion of stockholders' equity resulting form profitable business operation?

    A. Retained earnings
    B. Cash
    C. Accounts receivable
    D. Capital stock

    1.____

2. Which of the following is sued to compare revenues and expenses for a period of time in order to determine net income or loss?

    A. Balance sheet
    B. Owners' equity statement
    C. Statement of cash flows
    D. Income statement

    2.____

3. Accounting transactions are first recorded in the

    A. ledger
    B. trial balance
    C. journal
    D. T-account

    3.____

4. If net credit sales for a given year are $1.2 million and the average accounts receivable is $120,000, the average days to collect receivables is

    A. 10
    B. 30
    C. 36.5
    D. 71

    4.____

5. Each of the following is included in an end-of-period worksheet, EXCEPT

    A. financial statement information
    B. closing entries
    C. trial balance
    D. information for adjusting entries

    5.____

6. Generally accepted accounting principles suggest that a company's balance sheet show assets as the

    A. market value of the asset received in all cases
    B. cash equivalent value of what was given up or the asset received, whichever is more evident
    C. objective cost of external users
    D. cash outlay only, even if part of the consideration given was something other than cash

    6.____

7. At the end of the accounting period, Tripod Industries failed to make an adjusting entry to record depreciation. The effect of this omission will be an

   A. understatement of expenses
   B. understatement of assets
   C. overstatement of liabilities
   D. overstatement of revenues

8. On October 1, Agitpro paid three months' rent for office space. The payment was originally recorded in prepaid rent. Agitpro's adjusting entry on October 31 would include a

   A. debit to rent payable
   B. credit to rent expense
   C. debit to prepaid rent
   D. credit to prepaid rent

9. Beulah's Salon purchased a hair dryer on January 1 for $5,400. The dryer has a useful life of 10 years and a salvage value of $400. Using the double-declining balance method, calculate the depreciation expense for the second year of the dryer's useful life.

   A. $628
   B. $800
   C. $864
   D. $1026

10. The face amount of a bond, plus the unamortized premium, is referred to as its _____ value.

    A. carrying
    B. discounted
    C. par
    D. adjusted

11. Metabolon has a $10,000 credit balance in its allowance for doubtful accounts. During October it wrote off $4000 as uncollectible from a bankrupt customer. This entry will

    A. reduce owners' equity
    B. not affect the net income for the period
    C. increase total assets
    D. reduce total assets

12. A company uses a perpetual inventory system. When goods sold have been returned, the company should record the return with a

    A. debit to sales returns and allowances
    B. credit to inventory
    C. debit to cost of goods sold
    D. credit to sales returns and allowances

13. The objectives of financial reporting are met largely by each of the following, EXCEPT the

    A. cash flow statement
    B. federal income tax return

C. income statement
D. statement of financial position

14. _____ entries are used to zero out the balance in nominal accounts at the end of the period.

A. Reversing
B. Real
C. Closing
D. Adjusting

15. On October 1, Sterling Enterprises borrowed $100,000 from the bank. The loan is to be repaid in total in six months. The interest rate is 9%. On November 30, Sterling's total liability for this loan will be

A. $100,000
B. $101,500
C. $104,500
D. $109,000

16. Which of the following is shown on a bank statement?
   I. Deposits in transit
   II. Beginning and ending balances of the depositor's checking account
   III. Petty cash amounts
   IV. Outstanding checks

A. I and II
B. II only
C. I, II and IV
D. I, II, III and IV

17. Navanax had 25,000 shares of 8% preferred stock, $100 par, and 250,000 shares of $1 par common stock outstanding throughout the year. Net income for the year was $1,100,000, and Navanax declared and distributed a cash dividend of $2 per share on its common stock. Earnings per share equaled

A. $1.60
B. $2.10
C. $3.60
D. $4.40

18. A 120-day note, dated March 25, has a maturity date of July

A. 22
B. 23
C. 24
D. 25

19. Of the following steps in the accounting cycle, which is performed FIRST?

A. Adjusting accounts
B. Preparing an adjusted trial balance
C. Posting
D. Closing temporary accounts

Questions 20 and 21 refer to the following information: On March 1, Richie Corporation bought land by signing a note payable to the bank.

20. The March 1 journal entry would include a debit to the _____ account.   20._____

    A. revenue
    B. owners' equity
    C. liability
    D. asset

21. The March 1 journal entry would include a credit to the _____ account.   21._____

    A. liability
    B. asset
    C. owners' equity
    D. expense

22. A company's _____ activities are transactions with creditors to borrow money and/or   22._____
    repay the principal amounts of loans reported as cash flows.

    A. leveraging
    B. financing
    C. investing
    D. operating

23. Under the direct write-off method of accounting for uncollectible assets,   23._____

    A. the matching principle is illustrated by the relationship between current period net sales and current period uncollectible accounts
    B. when specific accounts receivable are determined to be worthless, the allowance for doubtful accounts is debited
    C. accounts receivable are not recorded in the balance sheet at net realizable value, but in the balance of the accounts receivable ledger account
    D. the uncollectible accounts expense is less than the expense would be under the income statement approach

24. The true interest rate of a note, computed only on the remaining balance of the unpaid   24._____
    debt for the specific time period, is known as the _____ interest rate.

    A. adjusted
    B. annual effective
    C. net
    D. annual compounded

25. An accountant is using the indirect method to calculate and report the net cash provided   25._____
    or used by operating activities. Under this method the accountant will have to adjust net income for

    I. revenues and expenses that did not provide or use cash
    II. changes in noncash current assets and current liabilities related to operating activities
    III. changes in current liabilities related to operating activities
    IV. gains and losses from investing and financing activities

A. I and II
B. I, II and III
C. II, III and IV
D. I, II, III and IV

KEY (CORRECT ANSWERS)

1. A
2. D
3. C
4. C
5. B

6. B
7. A
8. D
9. C
10. A

11. B
12. A
13. B
14. C
15. B

16. B
17. C
18. B
19. A
20. D

21. A
22. C
23. C
24. B
25. D

TEST 3

DIRECTIONS: Each question or incomplete statement is followed by several suggested answers or completions. Select the one that BEST answers the question or completes the statement. *PRINT THE LETTER OF THE CORRECT ANSWER IN THE SPACE AT THE RIGHT.*

1. An accountant is using the allowance method of recording bad debts. The journal entry to record the bad debts adjustment would

    A. debit the allowance for doubtful accounts
    B. credit the allowance for doubtful accounts
    C. debit accounts receivable
    D. credit accounts receivable

    1.____

2. The primary consumers of financial accounting information are

    A. investors and creditors
    B. corporate boards of directors
    C. financial managers
    D. budget officers

    2.____

3. The balance sheet of Fred's Fancies, a retailer, includes equipment, accounts receivable, cash, accounts payable, supplies, capital stock, notes payable, and notes receivable. This balance sheet contains _____ assets and _____ liabilities.

    A. 5; 2
    B. 5; 3
    C. 4; 4
    D. 6; 1

    3.____

4. The cost principle requires assets such as land, buildings, and equipment be recorded at

    A. appraisal value at the time of purchase
    B. appraisal value at the balance sheet date
    C. historical cost
    D. fair market value

    4.____

5. Each of the following would affect the book side of a bank reconciliation, EXCEPT

    A. a bank debit memorandum
    B. bank service charges
    C. outstanding checks
    D. a check-printing fee from the bank

    5.____

6. Ichthys Dive Shops borrowed $300,000 cash from the bank by signing a 5-year, 8% installment note. Given that the present value factor of an 8% annuity for 5 years is 3.9927 and each payment is $75,137, the present value of the note is

    A. $75,137
    B. $94,013
    C. $300,000
    D. $375,685

    6.____

2 (#3)

7. Before any year-end adjusting entries were made, the Tansu Mill's net income was $40,000. The following adjustments need to be made:

   Portion of insurance expiring $300
   Interest accrued on company savings $110
   Fees collected in advance now earned $2,400

   The income statement for the current year should show a net income of

   A. $37,410
   B. $38,010
   C. $41,990
   D. $42,210

8. If a substantial amount of a company's accounts payable are paid in cash, the company's current ratio would

   A. increase
   B. decrease
   C. remain the same
   D. change depending on the relationship between the payables and the current liabilities

9. Superscrubbers began providing janitorial services for a large corporation on January 15 for a monthly fee of $10,000. The first payment is to be received on February 15. The adjusting entry made by Superscrubbers on January 31 includes a

   A. debit of $5000 to janitorial fees receivable
   B. credit of $5000 to janitorial fees earned
   C. credit of $10,000 to janitorial fees earned
   D. debit of $5000 to unearned janitorial fees

10. Which of the following would NOT be closed during the closing process?

    A. Advertising expense
    B. Dividends
    C. Interest revenue
    D. Accumulated depreciation

11. The _____ principle requires that every business be accounted for separately and distinctly from its owner or owners.

    A. realization
    B. objectivity
    C. business entity
    D. compartmentalization

12. Funky Chic Decorating purchased a window treatment display for $25,000 and sold it several years later for $12,000. The original estimated residual value was $10,000, and the accumulated depreciation at the time of sale was $8000. The sale should be recorded as a

    A. $3000 loss
    B. $5000 loss

C. $2000 gain
D. $3000 gain

13. During a period of falling prices, the _____ method of inventory valuation will generally result in the highest amount of income taxes paid. 13.____

    A. first in, first out (FIFO)
    B. last in, first out (LIFO)
    C. gross profit
    D. weighted average

14. Which of the following statements about retained earnings is FALSE? 14.____

    A. They are not subject to statutory restrictions.
    B. They usually approximate a company's cumulative net income less dividends declared.
    C. They may be subject to appropriations by corporate directors for the purpose of limiting dividends.
    D. They may be subject to restrictions due to loan agreements.

15. On August 11 of the current year, Trachtenberg Corporation concluded that a customer's $8700 account receivable was uncollectible, and wrote the account off. Assuming the allowance method is used to account for bad debts, the write-off will 15.____

    A. have no effect on either net income or total assets
    B. decrease net income, but have no effect on total assets
    C. have no effect on net income, but decrease total assets
    D. decrease both net income and total assets

16. Chuzzlewit Enterprises sold equipment for $30,000. The cost was $70,000, and the equipment had accumulated depreciation of $50,000 at the time of the sale. In the investing section of the cash flow statement, the amount of _____ would be entered for this transaction. 16.____

    A. $0 (no entry)
    B. $10,000
    C. $20,000
    D. $30,000

Questions 17-19 refer to the following information: Multiplastics purchased a machine in January 1 that cost $300,000, has a residual value of $20,000, and a useful life of seven years.

17. The amount of depreciation expense for the second year, under the double-declining balance method, would be 17.____

    A. $47,287
    B. $53,576
    C. $61,261
    D. $85,800

18. The amount of depreciation expense for the third year, under the sum-of-the-years'-digits method, would be 18.____

A. $50,000
B. $53,576
C. $63,567
D. $70,000

19. The net book value of the machine at the end of the fourth year (after recording fourth-year depreciation), using the straight-line method, would be

   A. $120,000
   B. $140,000
   C. $171,429
   D. $188,888

20. The purpose of a classified balance sheet is to

   A. organize assets and liabilities into important subgroups
   B. show revenues, expenses, and net income
   C. report operating, investing, and financing activities
   D. measure a company's ability to pay its bills in a timely manner

21. What is the term for an expense resulting from a failure to take advantage of cash discounts on purchases?

   A. Trade discounts
   B. Shortfall
   C. Sales discounts
   D. Discounts lost

22. Accounts that appear on a postclosing trial balance are referred to as _____ accounts.

   A. projected
   B. real
   C. prorata
   D. nominal

23. Which of the following is an example of an operating activity?

   A. Purchasing office equipment
   B. Paying wages
   C. Selling stock
   D. Borrowing money from a bank

24. Landshark Corporation has operated with a gross profit rate of 30% for the last several years. On January 1 of the current year the company had an inventory with a cost of $50,000. Purchases of merchandise during January amounted to $60,000, and sales for the month were $90,000. Using the gross profit method, the estimated inventory on January 31 is

   A. $27,000
   B. $47,000
   C. $59,000
   D. $63,000

25. Earnings per share is an accounting item that is 25.____
    A. optional for most companies
    B. shown on the face of the income statement
    C. computed for both preferred and common stock
    D. expressed as "return on equity" in the ledger

KEY (CORRECT ANSWERS)

1.	A	11.	C
2.	A	12.	B
3.	A	13.	B
4.	C	14.	A
5.	C	15.	A
6.	C	16.	D
7.	D	17.	C
8.	A	18.	A
9.	B	19.	B
10.	D	20.	A

21.	D
22.	B
23.	B
24.	B
25.	B

TEST 4

DIRECTIONS: Each question or incomplete statement is followed by several suggested answers or completions. Select the one that BEST answers the question or completes the statement. *PRINT THE LETTER OF THE CORRECT ANSWER IN THE SPACE AT THE RIGHT.*

1. After the Yan Company collects $10,000 of its notes receivable, total assets are

    A. increased by $10,000
    B. decreased by $10,000
    C. unchanged, but total liabilities are greater
    D. unchanged

2. Revenues, expenses, and owner's withdrawal accounts are examples of _____ accounts.

    A. real
    B. permanent
    C. temporary
    D. closing

3. At the end of the year, the owners' equity of Plebeian Enterprises is $240,000, and is equal to 75% of total liabilities. The amount of total assets is

    A. $80,000
    B. $320,000
    C. $420,000
    D. $560,000

4. The _____ ratio of a company shows the percent of total assets provided by creditors.

    A. total asset turnover
    B. acid
    C. return on total assets
    D. debt

5. Which of the following would be recorded as a current liability?

    A. Accrued wages payable
    B. Property taxes payable
    C. Vacation benefits
    D. Income taxes payable

Questions 6-9 refer to the following information:
Year-end inventory for the Standish Company, under the periodic inventory system, is $25,000. The inventory on the first day of the year was $20,000 and purchases made during the year cost $40,000. Purchase returns and allowances equaled $1500, transportation in cost $500, and net sales for the year totaled $75,000.

6. At year's end, the net cost of purchases for Standish was

    A. $38,500
    B. $39,000

C. $40,000
D. $40,500

7. At year's end, the cost of goods sold for Standish was

   A. $31,500
   B. $34,000
   C. $44,000
   D. $59,000

8. At year's end, the cost of goods available for sale for Standish was

   A. $34,000
   B. $44,000
   C. $59,000
   D. $64,000

9. At year's end, the gross margin on sales for Standish was

   A. $41,000
   B. $44,000
   C. $59,000
   D. $61,000

10. Which of the following is a common nonrecurring item on the income statement?

    A. Discontinued operations
    B. Operating income
    C. Cumulative effect of a change in accounting estimate
    D. Ordinary gains and losses

11. If a transaction causes an asset account to decrease, it may also result in an increase

    A. in the combined total of liabilities and stockholders' equity
    B. of an equal amount in another asset account
    C. in a liability account
    D. of an equal amount in a stockholders' equity account

12. Beverly Corp. had total operating expenses of $100,000 in the previous accounting period; depreciation of $2,000; and an increase in accrued liabilities of $5,000. The company's prepaid expenses at the beginning of the period were $18,000; at the ending, they were $12,000.

    What was the cash paid by Beverly Corp. for operating expenses?

    A. $87,000
    B. $91,000
    C. $99,000
    D. $101,000

13. The _____ method of inventory valuation identifies the invoice cost of each item in ending inventory to determine the cost assigned to that inventory.

A. specific identification
B. first in, first out (FIFO)
C. last in, first out (LIFO)
D. weighted-average

14. In which of the following situations would revenue be recognized?

    A. An order is received with cash payment, and the order will be filled next month.
    B. An order has been shipped and will arrive at the customer's place of business after the end of the month. Shipping terms are FOB destination.
    C. An order has been received, and the goods have been set aside for the customer to pick up at her convenience.
    D. An order is received, and it will take about a week to manufacture enough goods to fill it.

15. A credit is used to record a(n)

    A. increase in an asset
    B. decrease in an expense
    C. increase in a liability
    D. increase in owners' equity

16. To balance the income statement columns of a worksheet, net income should be entered in the

    A. adjustments debit column
    B. balance sheet debit column
    C. income statement debit column
    D. income statement credit column

17. On May 1, Horticopia's accounts receivable totaled $6000. The allowance for doubtful accounts was $240. During the month of May, Horticopia made $20,000 in credit sales and collected $19,600 from its customers. On May 31, the not realizable value of accounts receivable is

    A. $6000
    B. $6160
    C. $6400
    D. $6640

18. Which of the following would affect the bank side of a bank reconciliation?

    A. Interest earned on a checking account
    B. Bank service charges
    C. Bank credit memorandum
    D. Deposits in transit

19. _____ preferred stock is a kind of stock on which the right to receive dividends is forfeited for any year in which dividends are not declared.

    A. Convertible
    B. Callable
    C. Noncumulative
    D. Cumulative

20. Which of the following are trade receivables?

    A. Deposits with creditors
    B. Cash advances to employees
    C. Amounts owed by customers on account
    D. Loans to affiliated companies

21. Which of the following is a term for the accounting procedure that estimates and reports bad debts expense from credit sales during the period of the sales, and also reports accounts receivable at the amount of cash proceeds that is expected from their collection?

    A. Adjustment method for uncollectible debts
    B. Aging of notes receivable
    C. Direct write-off method of accounting for bad debts
    D. Allowance method of accounting for bad debts

22. If Floracom accrues $200,000 for salaries payable at the end of the year,

    A. assets and owners' equity will remain unchanged
    B. assets decrease and liabilities increase by $200,000
    C. liabilities decrease and owners' equity increases by $200,000
    D. liabilities and expenses each increase $200,000

23. Each of the following is an operating activity, EXCEPT

    A. the purchase of equipment for cash
    B. the purchase of supplies for cash
    C. interest paid on a note payable
    D. cash sale

24. Compared to a perpetual inventory system, a periodic inventory system

    A. provides more timely information
    B. is based on estimates
    C. requires updating inventory-related accounts only at the end of each period
    D. allows a company to determine inventory and cost of goods sold at any time

25. On January 1, Uniqual Inc. purchased a machine for $60,000. The machine is estimated to have a useful life of 5 years and a salvage value of $10,000. Using the double-declining balance method of depreciation, what is the book value of the asset at the end of the year?

    A. $21,600
    B. $32,000
    C. $38,400
    D. $48,000

KEY (CORRECT ANSWERS)

1.	D	11.	B
2.	C	12.	A
3.	D	13.	A
4.	D	14.	C
5.	A	15.	B
6.	B	16.	C
7.	B	17.	B
8.	C	18.	D
9.	A	19.	C
10.	A	20.	C

21. D
22. D
23. A
24. C
25. A

EXAMINATION SECTION
TEST 1

DIRECTIONS: Each question or incomplete statement is followed by several suggested answers or completions. Select the one that BEST answers the question or completes the statement. *PRINT THE LETTER OF THE CORRECT ANSWER IN THE SPACE AT THE RIGHT.*

1. On the 2016 profit and loss statement of a firm, *Salaries* was listed as $15,250. The balance sheet on December 31, 2015 showed accrued salaries of $525; the balance sheet on December 31, 2016 showed prepaid salaries of $240 and accrued salaries of $600. During 2016, cash paid for salaries amounted to

   A. $15,250 B. $15,085 C. $14,890 D. $15,415

   1.____

2. B began business March 15 with a cash investment of $25,000. The records show:
   - Sales for the balance of the year — $56,000
   - Accounts Receivable, 12/31 — 30,000
   - Accounts Payable, 12/31 — 20,000
   - Inventory, 12/31 — 24,000
   - Gross profit mark-up on selling price, 25%

   The TOTAL cost of merchandise purchased during the year was

   A. $42,000 B. $66,000 C. $20,000 D. $44,000

   2.____

3. In the problem above, the cash balance on December 31 was

   A. $81,000 B. $51,000 C. $5,000 D. $9,000

   3.____

4. After Mr. S had been in business for a year, he ascertained the following facts:
   - Sales — $80,000
   - Raw materials used during the year at cost — 30,000
   - Labor — 50,000
   - Overhead — 8,000
   - Work-in-process inventory, 12/31, at cost — 18,000
   - Finished goods inventory, 12/31, at selling price — 25,000

   Assume that the mark-up has remained constant.
   The cost of manufacturing goods during the year was

   A. $70,000
   C. $63,000
   B. $88,000
   D. none of the above

   4.____

5. In the problem above, the selling price of the goods manufactured during the year was

   A. $50,000 B. $55,000 C. $80,000 D. $105,000

   5.____

6. The furniture and fixtures account of a firm showed a balance on December 31, 2016 of $9,500; the reserve for depreciation, furniture, and fixtures showed a balance of $6,540. Depreciation has been taken at 10% per annum, straight-line method. On April 1, 2016, a new machine was purchased for $500, for which an old machine, originally purchased for $300 on October 1, 2013, was traded in with an allowance of $50, and the balance of $450 was paid in cash. After making adjusting entries for 2016, the balance in the reserve account should be

   A. $7,505 B. $6,465 C. $7,430 D. $7,415

   6.____

2 (#1)

7. Graves, Owens, and Smith formed a partnership and invested $15,000 each. If the firm made a profit of $18,000 last year and profits and losses were shared equally, what was Owens' share of the net profit?

   A. $1,000   B. $5,000   C. $6,000   D. $9,000

8. Brooks and Carton are partners with an investment of $50,000 and $25,000, respectively.
   How much should be credited to Brooks as his share of a $60,000 profit if their agreement provides that the partners are to share profits and losses in proportion to their investments?

   A. $20,000   B. $30,000   C. $40,000   D. $50,000

9. The net worth of a corporation consisted of:
   Preferred stock - 6% cumulative participating par value $100 per
      share, 2000 shares outstanding $200,000
   Common stock - $50 par value, 3000 shares outstanding 150,000
   Retained earnings   70,000
   Common stockholders receive $3 a share after preferred stockholders receive 6% dividends; any remaining dividends are shared; $2 a share preferred, $1 a share common. Dividends have not yet been paid for the year.
   The book value of a share of common stock is

   A. $63.33   B. $73.33   C. $50   D. $60

10. Mr. D, the owner of a small coat concern, has had a bookkeeper keep the records of the firm, but has not employed an accountant. He hires you to correct the work of the bookkeeper. The schedule of accounts payable on December 31 is as follows:
    Ames $ 49
    Bates   740
    Cohen (debit balance)   18
    Other creditors   5000
    You discover the following:
       I. Mr. D has paid Mr. C $175 on the basis of his personal memory of the purchase. The bill for $175 had been entered incorrectly in the Purchase Journal as $157.
       II. A refund of $35 from B, the result of an overpayment, had been entered in the Accounts Receivable column of the Cash Receipts Journal and had been posted to B's account.
       III. Mr. D bought $300 worth of goods from A on September 5. The entry had been recorded in the Purchase Journal and posted. On October 8, A bought a $50 coat from Mr. D. The entry was recorded in the Sales Journal and posted to the customer's ledger. On October 11, Mr. D sent a check to A to settle with him. He allowed a 2% discount on the sale and, therefore, sent a check for $251. This was entered in the Accounts Payable column of the Cash Payments Journal. No other entry was made.
    The balance you found in the Accounts Payable account, before adjustments, was

    A. $5,740   B. $5,771   C. $5,701   D. $5,736

11. In the problem above, the balance in the Accounts Payable account after adjustments should be

    A. $5,670   B. $5,740   C. $5,789   D. $5,838

12. The balance of the Cash account in a firm's ledger on November 30 was $14,345 BEFORE consideration of the facts shown below.

    The following facts were disclosed:
    I. A $350 check was returned marked *Insufficient Funds*
    II. Collections made at the end of November, but not yet deposited, $2,125
    III. A bank debit memo for service charges, $5, was included with the bank statement
    IV. A check written for $75 was entered in the checkbook as $57
    V. Outstanding checks were:

#439	$ 76.00
#441	85.00
#442 (certified)	100.00
TOTAL	$261.00

    The bank statement on November 30 should show a balance of

    A. $12,708   B. $12,044   C. $12,008   D. $12,108

    12.____

KEY (CORRECT ANSWERS)

1. D
2. B
3. C
4. A
5. D
6. C
7. C
8. C
9. D
10. D
11. B
12. C

TEST 2

DIRECTIONS: Each question or incomplete statement is followed by several suggested answers or completions. Select the one that BEST answers the question or completes the statement. *PRINT THE LETTER OF THE CORRECT ANSWER IN THE SPACE AT THE RIGHT.*

1. The valuation account classified in the current assets section of the balance sheet is   1.___

   A. Allowance for Depreciation
   B. Reserve for Contingencies
   C. Allowance for Bad Debts
   D. Reserve for Discounts

2. The source for entries in the purchases journal is the purchase   2.___

   A. order
   B. requisition
   C. invoice
   D. memo

3. Insurance premiums paid on the lives of salaried officers of corporations, where the corporation is the beneficiary in case of death, are deductible expenses of the corporation PROVIDED that   3.___

   A. an appropriate increase in surrender value is shown as a credit to surplus
   B. life insurance premiums are not shown as expenses on corporate books
   C. life insurance premiums are charged to the *salaries* account of the officers
   D. a *loans payable* account is to be set up on the books

4. A transaction which will cause an increase in the net worth of a business is   4.___

   A. purchase of $1,000 merchandise for cash
   B. accommodation sale of $1,000 merchandise to a dealer
   C. loan of $1,000 made by the proprietor
   D. sale of $1,000 merchandise to a customer

5. Working capital is found by   5.___

   A. dividing current assets by current liabilities
   B. dividing current assets into current liabilities
   C. subtracting current liabilities from current assets
   D. subtracting current assets from current liabilities

6. The financial statement prepared for an estate, showing the sources from which the total cash to be distributed was obtained, is called a Statement of   6.___

   A. Variation of Net Profit
   B. Application of Funds
   C. Affairs
   D. Realization and Liquidation

7. The depreciated value of an asset based on replacement or appraised value is known as _____ value.   7.___

   A. book
   B. assessed
   C. net
   D. sound

8. The inventory method resulting in balance sheet figures which are CLOSEST to present cost is

   A. FIFO   B. LIFO   C. c/mkt   D. physical

9. Current assets $100,000; Fixed assets $50,000; Sales $200,000; Expenses $30,000; Current liabilities $40,000. The working capital turnover is

   A. $60,000   B. 2.5:1   C. 3.33   D. 20:3

10. The premium on a $75,000 fire insurance policy from January 1, 2015 to January 1, 2018 is $900. On December 30, 2015, there was a fire loss of $50,000, which was subsequently paid by the insurance company.
    The balance sheet value of the prepaid insurance on December 31, 2016 is

    A. $100   B. $150   C. $200   D. $400

11. F purchased an annuity policy at a total cost of $18,000. Starting on January 1, he began to receive an annual payment of $1,500. His life expectancy as of that date was 16 years. The amount of annuity income to be included in his gross income for the year on his Federal income tax return is

    A. $375   B. $540   C. $1125   D. $1500

12. The costs and expenses for the G Sales Co. for the year ended December 31 were:
    Fixed $100,000
    Variable $375,000
    The variable expenses were 75% of net sales.
    The break-even point is

    A. $500,000   B. $400,000   C. $475,000   D. $550,000

KEY (CORRECT ANSWERS)

1. C   7. D
2. C   8. B
3. A   9. C
4. D   10. A
5. C   11. A
6. D   12. B

EXAMINATION SECTION
TEST 1

DIRECTIONS: Each question or incomplete statement is followed by several suggested answers or completions. Select the one that BEST answers the question or completes the statement. *PRINT THE LETTER OF THE CORRECT ANSWER IN THE SPACE AT THE RIGHT.*

1. A long-term liability of a corporation is represented by

    A. stock certificates issued
    B. stock subscriptions received
    C. the balance of a sinking fund
    D. bonds issued

2. Which is an advantage of incorporating?

    A. Establishing good will
    B. Acquiring treasury stock
    C. Limiting the liability of the owners
    D. Avoiding governmental control

3. Undistributed profits of a corporation are shown in the _____ account.

    A. earned surplus
    B. treasury stock
    C. capital stock
    D. bonds payable

4. The TOTAL amount of equity, or ownership, in a corporation is found by adding

    A. treasury stock and surplus
    B. capital stock and subscriptions
    C. capital stock and surplus
    D. capital stock and good will

5. On January 1, 2018, the earned surplus account of the Kalfur Corporation had a credit balance of $42,300. The net income for 2018 (after taxes) was $12,500. The dividends declared for 2018 amounted to $8,400.
   The balance of the earned surplus account on December 31, 2018 after the books were closed was

    A. $4,100   B. $33,900   C. $38,200   D. $46,400

6. The State Disability Benefits Insurance law provides benefits for an employee or his family when the employee

    A. dies
    B. retires
    C. is temporarily unable to work because of an off-the-job accident
    D. is temporarily unable to work because of an on-the-job accident

7. Which account does NOT belong in the current liability section of a balance sheet? _____ payable.

    A. Interest   B. Notes   C. Accounts   D. Mortgage

8. If the merchandise inventory on hand at the end of 2018 was overstated, what would be the effect?

   A. Understatement of income for 2018
   B. Overstatement of income for 2018
   C. Understatement of assets at the end of 2018
   D. No effect on income or assets

9. The face value of a 45-day, 6% promissory note is $740. The maturity value of the note will be

   A. $734.45   B. $740.00   C. $745.55   D. $747.40

10. When cash is received as a result of sales, the PROPER business procedure is to

    A. put the cash in the petty cash box
    B. deposit the cash in a checking account at the end of the day
    C. deposit the cash in a savings account at the end of the day
    D. use the cash to pay current bills

11. Which item can be determined from information on the Income Statement (Profit and Loss Statement)?

    A. Working capital
    B. Rate of merchandise turnover
    C. Total liabilities
    D. Owner's worth

12. Which item belongs on the Income Statement for the year?

    A. B. Rand, Drawing
    B. Accrued Salaries, Payable
    C. Purchases Discount
    D. Allowance for Depreciation of Furniture and Fixtures

13. _____ tax is affected by the number of exemptions claimed.

    A. FICA
    B. State unemployment insurance
    C. State income tax
    D. Federal unemployment insurance

14. The source of an entry in the Cash Payments Journal is a

    A. sales invoice   B. checkbook stub
    C. petty cash voucher   D. general ledger

15. If a partnership agreement does not indicate how profits and losses are to be divided, then they will be distributed

    A. equally
    B. in proportion to investment
    C. according to duties and responsibilities
    D. by a court

16. The two parties on a promissory note are known as the _____ and _____.

    A. drawee; maker   B. drawee; drawer
    C. payee; drawee   D. payee; maker

17. In order to find the correct available cash balance when reconciling the checkbook balance with the bank balance, outstanding checks should be _____ balance.

    A. added to the checkbook   B. subtracted from the checkbook
    C. added to the bank   D. subtracted from the bank

18. A check drawn by a bank on funds that it has on deposit in another bank is known as a

    A. bank draft   B. certified check
    C. cashier's check   D. money order

19. _____ tax is contributed by the employee and matched by the employer.

    A. State unemployment insurance   B. State income tax
    C. FICA   D. Federal unemployment insurance

20. Which general ledger account would appear in a post-closing trial balance?

    A. Interest Income   B. Notes Receivable
    C. Sales Discount   D. Bad Debts Expense

21. A time draft frequently used in connection with a purchase of merchandise is a

    A. trade acceptance   B. check
    C. cashier's check   D. bank draft

22. A list of accounts and their balances prepared from a subsidiary ledger is called a

    A. statement of account   B. trial balance
    C. balance sheet   D. schedule

23. A time draft which states on its face that it resulted from the sale or purchase of merchandise is called a

    A. promissory note   B. purchase order
    C. bank draft   D. trade acceptance

24. A truck is purchased for $14,800. It is estimated that the truck will be used for four years. At the end of the four years, it is estimated that the truck will have a scrap value of $10,900.
    The amount of annual depreciation is

    A. $3,900   B. $1,425   C. $1,200   D. $975

25. The current ratio is found by

    A. *dividing* current assets by current liabilities
    B. *subtracting* current liabilities from current assets
    C. *subtracting* total liabilities from total assets
    D. *dividing* current assets by net income

KEY (CORRECT ANSWERS)

1. D
2. C
3. A
4. C
5. D

6. C
7. D
8. B
9. C
10. B

11. B
12. C
13. C
14. B
15. A

16. D
17. D
18. A
19. C
20. B

21. A
22. D
23. D
24. D
25. A

TEST 2

DIRECTIONS: Each question or incomplete statement is followed by several suggested answers or completions. Select the one that BEST answers the question or completes the statement. *PRINT THE LETTER OF THE CORRECT ANSWER IN THE SPACE AT THE RIGHT.*

1. The Federal individual income tax return must be filed by 1.____

    A. December 31 B. March 15
    C. April 15 D. June 30

2. When a firm discounts its own note at a bank, the account to be credited is 2.____

    A. Cash
    B. Notes Payable
    C. Notes Receivable Discounted
    D. Accounts Payable

3. Brooks and Carton are partners with an investment of $50,000 and $25,000, respectively. 3.____
   How much should be credited to Brooks as his share of a $60,000 profit if their agreement provides that the partners are to share profits and losses in proportion to their investments?

    A. $20,000   B. $30,000   C. $40,000   D. $50,000

4. At the end of the month, the total of the Schedule of Accounts Payable should equal the 4.____

    A. total of the Purchases column in the Purchases Journal
    B. total of the Accounts Payable column in the Cash Payments Journal
    C. balance of the Accounts Payable account in the General Ledger
    D. balance of the Purchases account in the General Ledger

5. When depreciation on a fixed asset is recorded, the effect of the entry on the fundamental bookkeeping equation is that the 5.____

    A. assets and capital remain unchanged
    B. assets increase; capital decreases
    C. assets decrease; capital decreases
    D. assets decrease; capital increases

6. The ORIGINAL source of an entry in the Purchases Journal is a 6.____

    A. purchase invoice B. stock inventory card
    C. purchase order D. creditor's account

7. The business form which is sent to each customer at the end of the month summarizing the transactions with him is called a 7.____

    A. schedule B. statement of account
    C. sales invoice D. voucher

8. When we receive a bank draft from a customer, our bookkeeper should debit 8.____

    A. Notes Payable B. Notes Receivable
    C. Accounts Receivable D. Cash

2 (#2)

9. The gross sales of a business are $170,000 and Sales Returns and Allowances $450. It is estimated that an additional allowance of 1% of net sales will be required. The amount listed for Bad Debts Expense on the Income Statement should be

    A. $1,250   B. $1,695.50   C. $1,700   D. $1,704.50

9._____

10. Which group of accounts will appear on a post-closing trial balance?

    A. Assets, liabilities, and expenses
    B. Income and expenses
    C. Liabilities, capital, and income
    D. Assets, liabilities, and capital

10._____

Questions 11-16.

DIRECTIONS: Questions 11 through 16 are to be answered SOLELY on the basis of the last part of the bank statement below, mailed to Arthur Greene for the month of June.

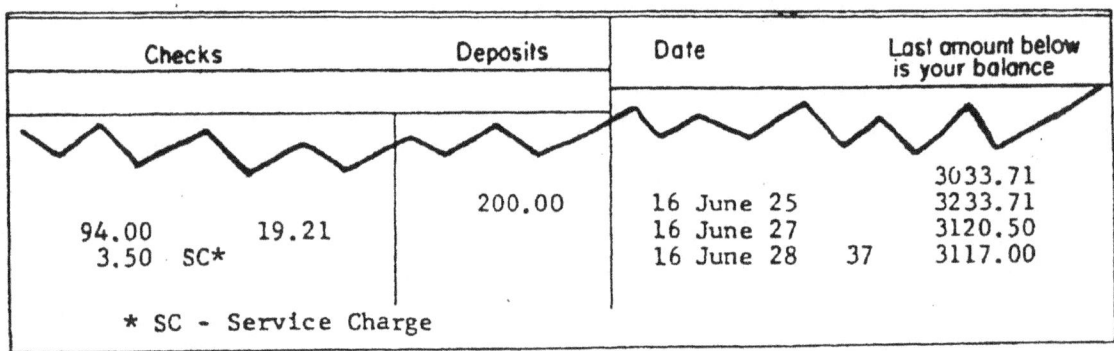

All the checks written have been paid except four. The last check written in June is No. 316. The stubs for the four outstanding checks are:

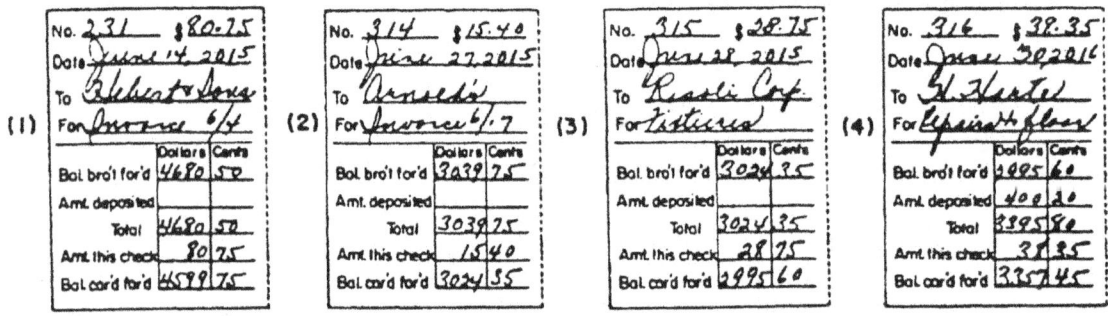

11. From the information available, what was Greene's corrected checkbook balance on June 30?

    A. $3,357.45   B. $3,117.00
    C. $3,353.95   D. $3,120.50

11._____

12. Which is the BEST reason that the deposit of $400.20, shown on Stub No. 316, does not appear on the bank statement?   12.____

    A. The bank has made an error.
    B. The bank has not credited his account.
    C. The withdrawals equal the deposits.
    D. The checks included in the deposit have not cleared the banks on which they were written.

13. When he examined the checks returned by his bank, Greene discovered that a check he had written for $44 had been incorrectly entered on the stub as $24.
    He should correct this error by   13.____

    A. adding $20 to his checkbook balance
    B. notifying his bank to add $20 to his account
    C. subtracting $20 from his checkbook balance
    D. subtracting $24 from his checkbook balance

14. On May 25, Greene wrote and had his bank certify a check for $150, which he mailed to Garcia, the payee. Garcia received the check on May 27 and deposited it in his bank on June 1. It was presented to Greene's bank and cleared for payment on June 2.
    On which date did Greene's bank deduct the $150 from his account?   14.____

    A. May 25   B. May 27   C. June 1   D. June 2

15. The journal entry to record the bank service charge shown on the bank statement should be made in the   15.____

    A. Petty Cashbook   B. General Journal
    C. Cash Receipts Journal   D. Cash Payments Journal

16. Greene's bookkeeper should prepare a bank reconciliation for June MAINLY to determine   16.____

    A. possible errors by comparing Greene's checkbook balance with the bank balance
    B. the total amount of checks written during the month
    C. which checks are still outstanding
    D. the total amount of cash deposited during the month

17. Which statement concerning a check is MOST accurate?   17.____

    A. A canceled check may be used to prove payment.
    B. Two signatures are required on each check drawn on a joint checking account.
    C. The corporation's name should be signed on the signature line of a check.
    D. Checks mailed for deposit should be endorsed by means of a blank endorsement.

18. If a check which has been certified is not used, which is the RECOMMENDED business practice?   18.____

    A. Mark the check *Void* and add the amount to the checkbook balance.
    B. Send a *stop payment* order to the bank.
    C. Deposit the check.
    D. Destroy the check.

4 (#2)

19. Ames' bank returned a check which he had deposited, marked *N.S.F.* This notation indicates that the

    A. check has been improperly endorsed
    B. drawer has overdrawn his bank account
    C. drawer has stopped payment on the check
    D. signature on the check has been forged

20. In order to determine the correct available bank balance, the amount of a deposit made, but not yet recorded in an account, should be _____ balance.

    A. *added* to the checkbook
    B. *added* to the bank balance
    C. *subtracted* from the checkbook
    D. *subtracted* from the bank

Questions 21-25.

DIRECTIONS: Questions 21 through 25 are to be answered on the basis of the following depreciation record.

DEPRECIATION RECORD

Delivery Truck	Tractson	04387A	July 1, 2015
Asset	Make	Number	Acquired
$4,000	5 years	$500	straight-line
Cost	Estimated Life	Salvage Value	Meth. of Depr.

Year	1st quarter	2nd quarter	3rd quarter	4th quarter
1			$175	$175
2	...	...	$175	$175
3	$175	$175		
4	$175			
5				
6				

21. According to the record, the LAST adjusting entry had been made on or about

    A. June 1, 2015 B. June 1, 2016
    C. December 31, 2016 D. March 31, 2017

22. The book value on the date of the latest entry is

    A. $500   B. $2,275   C. $2,775   D. $3,500

23. The TOTAL amount of depreciation which would be recorded during the lifetime of the truck is

    A. $4,500   B. $4,000   C. $3,500   D. $500

24. What is the annual rate of depreciation for the truck?

    A. 17.5%   B. 2%   C. 20%   D. 5%

25. If a business uses the straight-line method of depreciation, which is CORRECT? 25._____
    A. All assets are depreciated at the same rate.
    B. The older the asset, the greater the amount of depreciation recorded each year.
    C. The rate of depreciation is the same each year for a particular asset.
    D. The salvage value will be the same for all fixed assets.

KEY (CORRECT ANSWERS)

1.	C	11.	C
2.	B	12.	B
3.	C	13.	C
4.	C	14.	A
5.	C	15.	D
6.	A	16.	A
7.	B	17.	A
8.	D	18.	C
9.	B	19.	B
10.	D	20.	B

21. D
22. C
23. C
24. A
25. C

TEST 3

DIRECTIONS: Each question or incomplete statement is followed by several suggested answers or completions. Select the one that BEST answers the question or completes the statement. *PRINT THE LETTER OF THE CORRECT ANSWER IN THE SPACE AT THE RIGHT.*

1. Entries in the Cash Payments Journal are USUALLY recorded from

    A. purchase invoices
    B. check stubs
    C. cancelled checks
    D. expense sheets

    1.____

2. A bank draft received from a customer is recorded in the

    A. General Journal
    B. Note Register
    C. Sales Journal
    D. Cash Receipts Journal

    2.____

3. When sales taxes are collected from cash customers, the account credited is

    A. Sales Tax Payable
    B. Sales Tax
    C. Cash
    D. Accounts Payable

    3.____

4. One advantage of the corporate form of business is

    A. limited life
    B. limited capital
    C. limited liability
    D. dissolution on death of an officer

    4.____

5. Current assets minus current liabilities equals

    A. current turnover
    B. current ratio
    C. asset ratio
    D. working capital

    5.____

6. What is the LATEST date that an invoice dated October 15 with terms net 10 E.O.M. should be paid?

    A. October 25
    B. October 31
    C. November 10
    D. November 30

    6.____

7. The deduction allowed to a customer for an early payment of his account is known as a

    A. cash discount
    B. mark down
    C. credit memorandum
    D. trade discount

    7.____

8. In a C.O.D. freight shipment, the business form that the seller attaches to the bill of lading is a

    A. sight draft
    B. promissory note
    C. check
    D. time draft

    8.____

9. The form prepared to test the equality of debits and credits in the General Ledger is called

    A. statement of account
    B. balance sheet
    C. trial balance
    D. income statement

    9.____

10. If the depreciation of a truck is calculated by the straight-line method, which statement is CORRECT?

    A. As the truck becomes older, the rate of depreciation increases.
    B. The rate of depreciation is the same each year.
    C. The amount of annual depreciation is based on the truck's mileage.
    D. On a statement of profit and loss, the depreciation appears as a deferred expense.

11. A computer program used to create spreadsheets, graphs and charts, and maintain financial records is

    A. Quickbooks
    B. Adobe Reader
    C. Microsoft Powerpoint
    D. Microsoft Excel

12. An inventory of merchandise prepared from an actual count of stock items on hand is described as a(n) _____ inventory.

    A. perpetual   B. physical   C. estimated   D. fixed

13. Which is NOT classified as a current asset on the balance sheet?

    A. Petty Cash
    B. Notes Receivable
    C. Land
    D. Accounts Receivable

14. Which error will cause a trial balance to be out of balance?

    A. Failure to post the debit part of a journal entry
    B. Failure to record an entire journal entry
    C. Error in totaling the sales journal
    D. Posting a debit in the debit side of the wrong account

15. If a customer's check which you had deposited is returned to you by the bank labeled *dishonored*, what entry would be made?
    Debit

    A. Cash and credit customer's account
    B. Miscellaneous Expense and credit Cash
    C. customer's account and credit Capital
    D. customer's account and credit Cash

16. The total of the Purchases Journal for the month of May was incorrectly computed as $6,500. The correct amount was $5,500. The $6,500 was used to record and post the summary entry for the month.
    To correct the error, the bookkeeper should debit

    A. Merchandise Purchases and credit Accounts Payable $5,500
    B. Merchandise Purchases and credit Accounts Payable $1,000
    C. Accounts Payable and credit Merchandise Purchases $1,000
    D. Accounts Payable and credit Merchandise Purchases $6,500

17. Entries in the Purchases Journal are USUALLY recorded from

    A. purchase requisitions
    B. purchase invoices
    C. check stubs
    D. credit memorandums

18. Merchandise was sold on April 10, 2018 for $400 less a trade discount of 25%, terms 2/10, n/30.
    The amount required to settle the invoice on April 20 is

    A. $294   B. $300   C. $392   D. $400

    18._____

19. When the books were closed at the end of the business fiscal year, there was a failure to record depreciation on Office Equipment for the year.
    This error had the effect of

    A. *understating* the book value of the asset Office Equipment
    B. *overstating* the book value of the asset Office Equipment
    C. *understating* the net income of the asset Office Equipment
    D. *overstating* operating expenses

    19._____

Questions 20-25.

DIRECTIONS: Questions 20 through 25 are to be answered SOLELY on the basis of the following bank reconciliation statement.

```
CONDON, INC.   Bank Reconciliation   March 31.

Checkbook balance         $3,148.70    Bank Balance                      $3,830.65
Less: Service Charge           4.15    Add: Deposit in
                                            Transit                         310.00
                                       Total                              4,140.65
                                       Less: Outstanding
                                             Checks
                                             No. 815  $470.20
                                                 817   525.90               996.10
                                       (No. 813 certified
                                                       920.00)
Adjusted checkbook balance $3,144.55   Available
                                       bank balance                      $3,144.55
```

20. Which entry will be made on the books of Condon, Inc. to record the bank service charge?
    Debit

    A. Cash, credit Bank Charges
    B. Bank Charges, credit Accounts Payable
    C. Bank Charges, credit Cash
    D. Bank Account, credit Bank Charges

    20._____

21. The deposit in transit of $310 will be listed on the

    A. bank statement for the month of March
    B. bank statement for the month of April
    C. bank statement for the month of February
    D. check stub record *only*

    21._____

22. The bookkeeper determined which checks were outstanding by

    A. counting the cancelled checks
    B. examining the bank statement
    C. comparing the cancelled checks with the bank statement
    D. comparing the cancelled checks with the check stubs

23. The certified check of $920 was NOT deducted with the other outstanding checks because it

    A. was deducted from our bank balance at the time it was certified
    B. was not deducted from our checkbook balance when it was written
    C. will not be cashed by our bank
    D. will not be deducted from our bank balance until it clears our bank

24. The MAIN reason for preparing the bank reconciliation statement is to determine the

    A. total amount of cancelled checks
    B. total amount of outstanding checks
    C. total deposits with withdrawals for the month
    D. errors that might have been made

25. A trial balance is prepared to

    A. see if the totals agree with the subsidiary ledgers
    B. see if the total debit balances in the General Ledger agree with the total credit balances in the General Ledger
    C. show the worth of the business
    D. make up statements of customers' accounts

KEY (CORRECT ANSWERS)

1.	B	11.	D
2.	D	12.	B
3.	A	13.	C
4.	C	14.	A
5.	D	15.	D
6.	C	16.	C
7.	A	17.	B
8.	A	18.	A
9.	C	19.	B
10.	B	20.	C

21. B
22. D
23. A
24. D
25. B

TEST 4

DIRECTIONS: Each question or incomplete statement is followed by several suggested answers or completions. Select the one that BEST answers the question or completes the statement. *PRINT THE LETTER OF THE CORRECT ANSWER IN THE SPACE AT THE RIGHT.*

1. The due date of a 60-day promissory note dated June 15 is August 1.____

   A. 13 B. 14 C. 15 D. 16

2. Using the information that can be found in the Income Statement, one can find the 2.____

   A. current ratio
   B. merchandise turnover
   C. working capital
   D. rate of return on capital

3. Which of the following is NOT a computer program commonly used for accounting and finance purposes? 3.____

   A. QuarkXPress B. Peachtree
   C. Quicken D. Quickbooks

4. The ABC Corporation has 100,000 shares of stock outstanding. The Corporation decides to distribute to the stockholders a $200,000 profit.
   If a stockholder owns 100 shares of stock, he will receive a TOTAL dividend of 4.____

   A. $50.00 B. $2.00 C. $200.00 D. $.50

5. A transaction that will cause a DECREASE in capital is a 5.____

   A. purchase of office equipment on credit
   B. payment of a creditor's account less a cash discount
   C. payment of an interest-bearing note
   D. prepayment of freight for a customer, to be charged to the customer's account

6. Mr. Davis is married and has three children who go to school. His oldest son, age 17, earned $900 during the year working parttime.
   On his joint Federal income tax return, Mr. Davis may claim a MAXIMUM of _____ exemptions. 6.____

   A. five B. two C. three D. four

7. If the total of the Schedule of Accounts Receivable does not agree with the balance in the Accounts Receivable Controlling account, the difference may have been caused by 7.____

   A. adding the Sales Journal incorrectly
   B. failing to enter a sale in the Sales Journal
   C. posting a sale to the wrong customer's account
   D. failing to record a check received from a customer

8. An entry in the general journal is USUALLY made from the 8.____

   A. sales invoice B. purchase invoice
   C. credit memorandum D. incoming check

40

9. An example of a tax collected by the Federal government is the 9.____

   A. sales tax
   B. real estate tax
   C. automobile registration fee
   D. social security tax

10. The adjusting entry at the end of the year to record the estimated depreciation for the year results in a(n) 10.____

    A. *increase* in liabilities and a decrease in capital
    B. *decrease* in assets and an increase in assets
    C. *decrease* in assets and a decrease in capital
    D. *decrease* in assets and an increase in capital

11. On December 28, the total in the Salaries Expense Account was $59,500. On December 31, the bookkeeper recorded accrued salaries of $600. 11.____
    The entry to close the Salaries Expense Account on December 31 should be debit the _____ and credit the _____.

    A. Income and Expense Summary Account for $59,500; Salaries Expense Account for $59,500
    B. Income and Expense Summary Account for $60,100; Salaries Expense Account for $60,100
    C. Income and Expense Summary Account for $58,900; Salaries Expense Account for $58,900
    D. Salaries Expense Account for $59,500; Income and Expense Summary Account for $59,500

12. The tax paid by the employee to provide benefits upon his retirement is the 12.____

    A. FICA tax
    B. State Disability Benefits
    C. Federal withholding tax
    D. workmen's compensation insurance

13. The Federal income tax form that is given to the employee to show his total salary for the year and the amount of withholding tax for the year is called Form 13.____

    A. 941   B. W-4   C. 1099   D. W-2

14. An error that would cause the trial balance to be out of balance would be INCORRECTLY adding 14.____

    A. the Purchase Journal
    B. the cash column in the Cash Receipts Journal
    C. the Schedule of Accounts Receivable
    D. extensions on an invoice

15. An account that would be shown in a post-closing trial balance is 15.____

    A. Notes Receivable   B. Sales Income
    C. Discount on Purchases   D. Freight Out

16. You have just posted an entry from the Sales Journal to the customer's account. The correct amount in the Sales Journal is $125, but you posted $12.50.
To correct the error, you should

    A. draw a single line through the $12.50 in the account and write $125 above it
    B. debit in the General Journal the customer's account for $112.50 and credit the Sales Income Account for $112.50
    C. credit in the General Journal the customer's account for $12.50 and debit the Sales Income Account for $12.50
    D. debit in the Sales Journal the customer's account for $112.50 and credit the Sales Income Account for $112.50

17. When the bookkeeper added the trial balance, she found that it did not balance.
To find the reason, a logical FIRST step would be to

    A. check the pencil footings in ledger accounts
    B. add the trial balance a second time
    C. check whether figures were copied correctly from the ledger to the trial balance
    D. check postings from the journals

18. A column or group of columns containing data of a specific nature on a punched card is called a

    A. zone   B. field   C. row   D. file

19. *Allowance for Doubtful Accounts* is BEST described as a(n) _____ account.

    A. contingent liability   B. capital
    C. expense   D. asset valuation

20. A sales invoice to Judy Burns for $50 was entered in the Sales Journal as $150.
Which would occur as a result of this error?
The

    A. trial balance will not balance at the end of the month
    B. balance of the monthly statement to Judy Burns will be overstated
    C. check received from Judy Burns in payment of her account will be larger than the correct amount
    D. Accounts Receivable controlling account will not agree with the Schedule of Accounts Receivable at the end of the month

21. Sales taxes which are collected from customers and which will subsequently be remitted to the State Tax Bureau are recorded by the retailer as a(n)

    A. operating expense in the Income Statement
    B. addition to sales in the Income Statement
    C. current asset in the Balance Sheet
    D. current liability in the Balance Sheet

22. When the payee of a check writes as an endorsement *Pay to the order of (name of the firm)* before his signature, he has used a _____ endorsement.

    A. blank   B. qualified
    C. restrictive   D. full

23. Entries in the Purchases Journal are USUALLY made from which source document?   23.____

    A. Purchase order
    B. Purchase requisition
    C. Incoming invoice
    D. Outgoing invoice

24. Which is shown on the bank statement sent by the bank each month?   24.____

    A. Outstanding checks
    B. Deposits in transit
    C. Checks paid by the bank during the month
    D. The amount of interest earned during the month

25. The authorization by the State of New York which permits a group of persons to do business as a corporation is called the   25.____

    A. charter
    B. by-laws
    C. trade acceptance
    D. articles of copartnership

KEY (CORRECT ANSWERS)

1.	B	11.	B
2.	B	12.	A
3.	A	13.	D
4.	C	14.	B
5.	C	15.	A
6.	A	16.	A
7.	A	17.	B
8.	C	18.	B
9.	D	19.	D
10.	C	20.	B

21. D
22. D
23. C
24. C
25. A

EXAMINATION SECTION
TEST 1

DIRECTIONS: Each question or incomplete statement is followed by several suggested answers or completions. Select the one that BEST answers the question or completes the statement. *PRINT THE LETTER OF THE CORRECT ANSWER IN THE SPACE AT THE RIGHT.*

Questions 1-5.

DIRECTIONS: Questions 1 through 5 are to be answered on the basis of the following information.

Assume that you are working in an agency and that you are requested to verify certain financial data with respect to the various business entities described below. This information is required to verify that tax returns and/or other financial reports submitted to your agency are correct.

In an auditing review of the income statements of several business firms (Companies X, Y, and Z), you find the financial information given below. Based upon the account balances shown, select the correct answer for the statement information requested.

1. Company X
   Sales $ 160,000
   Opening inventory $ 70,000
   Purchases $ 80,000
   Purchase returns $ 1,200
   Cost of goods sold $ 127,000
   The ending inventory based upon the above data is

   A. $21,800   B. $23,000   C. $24,200   D. $33,000

2. Company Y
   Opening inventory $ 50,000
   Purchases $ 145,000
   Ending inventory $ 28,500
   Gross profit $ 56,000
   Sales and administrative expenses $ 64,000
   Sales for the period based upon the above data are

   A. $110,500   B. $166,500   C. $222,500   D. $286,500

3. Company Z
   Sales for the period $ 200,000
   Net profit   7% of sales
   Purchases $ 180,000
   Ending inventory $ 70,000
   Gross profit $ 60,000
   Cost of goods sold for Company Z is

   A. $110,000   B. $140,000   C. $180,000   D. $250,000

45

4. The opening inventory of Company Z would be

   A. $10,000   B. $20,000   C. $30,000   D. $80,000

5. The operating expenses for Company Z would be

   A. $10,000   B. $14,000   C. $20,000   D. $46,000

Questions 6-8.

DIRECTIONS: Questions 6 through 8 are to be answered on the basis of the following information, which is taken from the books and records of a business firm.

```
Sales for the calendar year                $52,000
   Based upon FIFO Inventory:
      Goods available for sale             $46,900
      Inventory at December 31             $12,700

   Based upon LIFO Inventory:
      Goods available for sale             $46,900
      Inventory at December 31             $10,400
```

6. If FIFO Inventory valuation is used, the gross profit will be

   A. $5,100   B. $15,500   C. $17,800   D. $34,200

7. If LIFO Inventory valuation method is used, the gross profit will be

   A. $2,300   B. $15,500   C. $17,800   D. $36,500

8. If LIFO Inventory method is used, compared with the FIFO method, the cost of goods sold will be

   A. more by $2,300   B. less by $2,300
   C. more by $10,400   D. less by $12,700

9. Which one of the following would NOT properly be classified as an asset on the balance sheet of a business firm?

   A. Investment in stock of another firm
   B. Premium cost of a three-year fire insurance policy
   C. Cash surrender value of life insurance on life of corporate officer; policy is owned by the company and the company is the beneficiary
   D. Amounts owing to employees for services rendered

10. Which one of the following would NOT properly be classified as a current asset?

    A. Travel advances to salespeople
    B. Postage in a postage meter
    C. Cash surrender value of life insurance policy on an officer which policy names the corporation as the beneficiary
    D. Installment notes receivable due over 18 months in accordance with normal trade practice

11. Able, Baker, and Carr formed a partnership. Able contributed $10,000; Baker contributed $5,000; and Carr contributed an automobile with a fair market value of $5,000. They have no partnership agreement. The first year, the partnership earned $18,000. The partners will share the profits as follows: Able, _____; Baker, _____; Carr, _____.   11.____

   A. $9,000; $4,500; $4,500
   B. $6,000; $6,000; $6,000
   C. $12,000; $6,000; no share
   D. $8,000; $5,000; $5,000

Questions 12-13.

DIRECTIONS: Questions 12 and 13 are to be answered on the basis of the information below.

The XYZ partnership had the following balance sheet as of December 31:

Cash	$ 5,000
Other assets	40,000
Total	$45,000
Liabilities	$12,000
X Capital	20,000
Y Capital	10,000
Z Capital	3,000
Total	$45,000

The partners shared profits equally. They decided to liquidate the partnership at December 31.

12. If the other assets were sold for $52,000, each partner will be entitled to a final cash distribution of: 12.____
    X, _____; Y, _____; Z, _____.

    A. $15,000; $15,000; $15,000
    B. $24,000; $14,000; $7,000
    C. $20,000; $10,000; $3,000
    D. $23,000; $13,000; $6,000

13. If the other assets were sold for $31,000, each partner will be entitled to a final cash distribution of: 13.____
    X, _____; Y, _____; Z, _____.

    A. $14,000; $5,000; $5,000
    B. $8,000; $8,000; $8,000
    C. $15,000; $15,000; $15,000
    D. $17,000; $7,000; no cash share

14. Items selling for $40 for which there were 10% selling costs were purchased for inventory at $20 each. Selling prices and costs remained steady, but at the date of the financial statement the market price had dropped to $16. The inventory remaining from the original purchase was written down to $16.
    Of the following, it is CORRECT to state that the _____ overstated.

    A. cost of sales of the subsequent year will be
    B. current year's income is
    C. income of the following year will be
    D. closing inventory of the current year is

15. Dividends in arrears on a cumulative preferred stock should be reported on the balance sheet as

    A. an accrued liability
    B. restricted retained earnings
    C. an explanatory note
    D. a deduction from preferred stock

16. The effect of recording the payment of a 10% dividend paid in stock would be to

    A. *increase* the current ratio
    B. *decrease* the amount of working capital
    C. *increase* the total stockholder equity
    D. *decrease* the book value per share of stock outstanding

17. The owner of a truck which originally had cost $12,000 but now has a book value of $1,500 was offered $3,000 for it by a used truck dealer. However, the owner traded it in for a new truck listed at $19,000 and received a trade-in allowance of $4,000.
    The cost basis for the new truck following the Federal income tax rules properly amounts to

    A. $15,000   B. $16,000   C. $16,500   D. $17,500

18. In planning for purchases to be made during the next month, the following information is to be used:
    Budgeted sales for the month   73,000 units
    Inventory at beginning of the month   19,000 units
    Planned inventory at end of the month   14,000 units
    From the above information, the amount of units to be purchased is _____ units.

    A. 40,000   B. 59,000   C. 68,000   D. 78,000

19. A branch office of a company has the following plan:
    Cash balance at beginning of the month $ 10,000
    Planned cash balance at end of the month $ 15,000
    Expected receipts for the month $ 180,000
    Expected disbursements for the month $ 205,000
    In order to comply with this plan, the accountant should recommend that the branch obtain an additional allocation of

    A. $20,000   B. $25,000   C. $30,000   D. $50,000

20. A company uses the reserve method of bad debt expense and sets up a bad debt account at 2% of sales. The sales were $500,000. The company wrote off $7,500 in accounts receivable.
The effect of these entries on net income for the period is a(n)

A. $2,500 increase
B. $7,500 decrease
C. $8,000 decrease
D. $10,000 decrease

20.____

21. The Daled Corporation has applied to their bank for a $50,000 loan which they will need for 90 days. The bank grants the loan, which will be discounted at 7% interest (use a 360-day year).
The Daled Corporation will receive credit in their account at the bank for

A. $46,500   B. $49,125   C. $50,000   D. $50,875

21.____

Questions 22-25.

DIRECTIONS: Questions 22 through 25 are to be answered on the basis of the information below.

Assume that you are reviewing some accounts of a company and find the following: the Machinery Account and the Accumulated Depreciation - Machinery Account.

Machinery

Jan. 1, 2014	Machine #1	20,000	July 1, 2015	6,000
Jan. 1, 2015	Machine #2	16,000		
July. 1, 2015	Machine #3	12,000		
Jan. 1, 2017	Machine #4	20,000		

Accumulated Depreciation - Machinery

		Dec. 31, 2014	5,000
		Dec. 31, 2015	10,500

Machines are depreciated based upon a four-year life and using the straight-line method. Assume no salvage values.

On July 1, 2015 Machine #1, purchased on January 1, 2014, was sold for $6,000 cash. The bookkeeper debited Cash and credited Machinery for $6,000.

On January 1, 2017, Machine #2 was traded in for a newer model. The new machine had a list price of $34,000. A trade-in value of $10,000 was granted. $20,000 was paid in cash, and the bookkeeper debited Machinery and credited Cash for $20,000. Income tax rules should have been applied making this entry.

If any errors were made in recording the machine values or depreciation, you are asked to correct them and determine the corrected asset values and proper accumulated depreciation.

22. As of December 31, 2014, you determine that these two accounts   22._____

    A. are correct
    B. are incorrect
    C. overstate asset book values
    D. understate asset book values

23. As of December 31, 2015, you determine that to correct the Machinery Account balance   23._____
    you should leave it

    A. unchanged
    B. increased by $6,000
    C. decreased by $14,000
    D. decreased by $5,500

24. As of December 31, 2015, you determine that, to reflect the proper balance, the Accumulated Depreciation -Machinery account should   24._____

    A. remain unchanged
    B. be increased by $10,000
    C. be decreased by $10,000
    D. be decreased by $5,500

25. After the January 1, 2017 entry, you determine that the Machinery Account should properly   25._____

    A. remain unchanged
    B. reflect a corrected balance of $52,000
    C. reflect a corrected balance of $40,000
    D. reflect a corrected balance of $56,000

Questions 26-29.

DIRECTIONS: Questions 26 through 29 are to be answered on the basis of the information below.

Assume that you are assigned to prepare an Audit Report Summary on the L Company. The L Company uses the accrual method and has an accounting year ending December 31. The bookkeeper of the company has made the following errors:

1. A $1,500 collection from a customer was received on December 29, 2016, but not recorded until the date of its deposit in the bank, January 4, 2017.
2. A supplier's $1,900 invoice for inventory items received December 2016 was not recorded until January 2017. (Inventories at December 31, 2016 and 2017 were stated correctly, based on physical count.)
3. Depreciation for 2016 was understated by $700.
4. In September 2016, a $350 invoice for office supplies was charged to the Utilities Expense account. Office supplies are expensed as purchased.
5. December 31, 2016, sales on account of $2,500 were recorded in January 2017, although the merchandise had been shipped and was not in the inventory.

Assume that no other errors have occurred and that no correcting entries have been made. Ignore all income taxes.

26. After correcting the errors reported above, the corrected Net Income for 2016 was   26.____

   A. overstated by $100
   B. understated by $800
   C. understated by $1,800
   D. neither understated nor overstated

27. Working Capital on December 31, 2016 was   27.____

   A. understated by $600
   B. understated by $2,300
   C. understated by $1,200
   D. neither understated nor overstated

28. Total Assets on December 31, 2017 were   28.____

   A. overstated by $1,100
   B. overstated by $1,800
   C. understated by $850
   D. neither understated nor overstated

29. The cash balance was   29.____

   A. correct as stated originally
   B. overstated by $1,500
   C. understated by $2,500
   D. understated by $1,500

30. Currently preferred terminology for statements to be presented limits the use of the term   30.____
    reserve to

   A. an actual liability of a known amount
   B. estimated liabilities
   C. appropriations of retained earnings
   D. valuation (contra) accounts

KEY (CORRECT ANSWERS)

1. A	11. B	21. B
2. C	12. B	22. A
3. B	13. D	23. C
4. C	14. C	24. C
5. D	15. C	25. C
6. C	16. D	26. A
7. B	17. C	27. A
8. A	18. C	28. B
9. D	19. C	29. D
10. C	20. D	30. C

TEST 2

DIRECTIONS: Each question or incomplete statement is followed by several suggested answers or completions. Select the one that BEST answers the question or completes the statement. *PRINT THE LETTER OF THE CORRECT ANSWER IN THE SPACE AT THE RIGHT.*

Questions 1-4.

DIRECTIONS: Questions 1 through 4 are to be answered on the basis of the information below.

Salary expense was listed as a total of $27,600 for the month of June 2017. Withholding taxes were determined to be $7,250 for income taxes and $1,170 for FICA taxes withheld from employees. Payroll deductions for employee pension fund contribution amounted to $2,500.

Assume the employer's FICA tax share is equal to the employees' and that the employer's share of pension costs is double that of the employees and the employer also pays a 3% Unemployment Insurance Tax based upon $20,000 of the wages paid. The employer pays $1,500 for health insurance plans.

1. The amount of cash that must be obtained to meet this net payroll to pay employees is 1._____

   A. $16,680   B. $19,180   C. $20,350   D. $27,600

2. The total payroll tax expense for this payroll period is 2._____

   A. $1,170   B. $1,760   C. $2,340   D. $2,940

3. The total liability for withholding and payroll taxes payable is 3._____

   A. $2,340   B. $7,250   C. $8,420   D. $10,190

4. The expense of the employer for pension and health care fringe benefits is 4._____

   A. $1,500   B. $2,500   C. $5,000   D. $6,500

Questions 5-6.

DIRECTIONS: Questions 5 and 6 are to be answered on the basis of the following.

The Victory Corporation provides an incentive plan whereby its president receives a bonus equal to 10% of the corporate income in excess of $150,000. The bonus is based upon income before income taxes but after calculating the bonus.

5. If the income for the calendar year 2016, before income taxes and before the bonus, were $480,000 and the effective tax rate is 40%, the amount of the bonus would be 5._____

   A. $15,000   B. $30,000   C. $33,000   D. $48,000

6. The income tax expense for calendar year 2016 would be 6._____

   A. $60,000   B. $132,000   C. $180,000   D. $192,000

52

Questions 7-8.

DIRECTIONS: Questions 7 and 8 are to be answered on the basis of the information below.

A contract has been awarded to the low bidder. This contractor will then commence construction of a building for the total contract price of $30,000,000. The expected cost of construction is $27,510,000. You are given the additional facts:

	2017	2018	2019
Contract Price as above	$30,000,000	$30,000,000	$30,000,000
Actual Cost to Date	9,170,000	13,755,000	27,510,000
Estimated Cost to Complete	18,340,000	13,755,000	---
Estimated Total Cost	$27,510,000	$27,510,000	$27,510,000
Estimated Total Income Billings	2,490,000		
	$9,000,000	$9,000,000	$9,000,000

7. For 2017, the income to be recognized on a percentage of completion basis would be   7.____

 A. $830,000
 B. $2,490,000
 C. $3,000,000
 D. $9,000,000

8. For 2018, the income to be recognized by the contractor on a percentage of completion basis would be   8.____

 A. $415,000   B. $424,500   C. $830,000   D. $1,245,000

9. If the city borrows the $9,000,000 to pay the first billing for the contract above at 10% interest for two years, and the second $9,000,000 at 7% interest for one year, then the interest costs related to this building are approximately   9.____

 A. $630,000
 B. $1,800,000
 C. $2,430,000
 D. $3,000,000

10. The books of the Monmouth Corporation show the following: 10.____

	2016	2015	2014
Average earnings for prior 3 years	$70,000	$75,000	$78,000
Net tangible assets	$40,000	$42,000	$50,000

 If it is expected that 15% would be normal earnings on net tangible assets, then the average excess earnings are

 A. $7,120   B. $8,333   C. $9,800   D. $10,800

Questions 11-15.

DIRECTIONS: Questions 11 through 15 are to be answered on the basis of the information below.

3 (#2)

When balance sheets are analyzed, working capital always receives close attention. Adequate working capital enables a company to carry sufficient inventories, meet current debts, take advantage of cash discounts, and extend favorable terms to customers. A company that is deficient in working capital and unable to do these things is in a poor competitive position.

Below is a Trial Balance as of June 30, 2017, in alphabetical order, of the Worth Corporation.

	DEBITS	CREDITS
Accounts Payable		$ 50,000
Accounts Receivable	$ 40,000	
Accrued Expenses Payable		10,000
Capital Stock		10,000
Cash	20,000	
Depreciation Expense	5,000	
Inventory	60,000	
Plant & Equipment (net)	30,000	
Retained Earnings		20,000
Salary Expense	35,000	
Sales		100,000
	$190,000	$190,000

11. The Worth Corporation's Working Capital, based on the data above, is

    A. $50,000   B. $55,000   C. $60,000   D. $65,000

11.____

12. Which one of the following transactions *increases* Working Capital?

    A. Collecting outstanding accounts receivable
    B. Borrowing money from the bank based upon a 90-day interest-bearing note payable
    C. Paying off a 60-day note payable to the bank
    D. Selling merchandise at a profit

12.____

13. The Worth Corporation's Current Ratio, based on the data above, is

    A. 1.7 to 1   B. 2 to 1   C. 2.5 to 1   D. 4 to 3

13.____

14. Which one of the following transactions *decreases* the Current Ratio?

    A. Collecting an accounts receivable
    B. Borrowing money from the bank giving a 90-day interest-bearing note payable
    C. Paying off a 60-day note payable to the bank
    D. Selling merchandise at a profit

14.____

4 (#2)

15. The payment of a current liability, such as Payroll Taxes Payable, will   15.____

    A. *increase* the Current Ratio but have no effect on the Working Capital
    B. *increase* the Working Capital, but have no effect on the Current Ratio
    C. *decrease* both the Current Ratio and Working Capital
    D. *increase* both the Current Ratio and Working Capital

16. During the year 2016, the Camp Equipment Co. made sales to customers totaling $100,000 that were subject to sales taxes of $8,000. Net cash collections totaled $92,000. Discounts of $3,000 were allowed. During the year 2016, uncollectible accounts in the sum of $2,000 were written off the books.   16.____
The net change in accounts receivable during the year 2016 was

    A. $10,500   B. $11,000   C. $13,000   D. $13,500

17. The Cable Co. received a $6,000, 8%, 60-day note dated May 1, 2016 from a customer. On May 16, 2016, the Cable Co. discounted the note at 6% at the bank. The net proceeds from the discounting of the note amounted to   17.____

    A. $5,954.40   B. $6,034.40   C. $6,064.80   D. $6,080.00

18. In reviewing the customers' accounts in the Accounts Receivable ledger for the entire year 2016, the following errors are discovered: 18.____
    1. A sale in the amount of $500 to the J. Brown Co. was erroneously posted to the K. Brown Co.
    2. A sales return of $100 from the Gale Co. was debited to their account.
    3. A check was received from a customer, M. White and Co. in payment of a sale of $500 less 2% discount. The check was entered properly in the cash receipts book but was posted to the M. White and Co. account in the amount of $490.
The difference between the controlling account and its related accounts receivable schedule amounts to

    A. $90   B. $110   C. $190   D. $210

19. Assume that you are called upon to audit a cash fund. You find in the cash drawer postage stamps and I.O.U.'s signed by employees, totaling together $425. In preparing a financial report, the $425 should be reported as   19.____

    A. petty cash
    B. investments
    C. supplies and receivables
    D. cash

20. On December 31, 2016, before adjustment, Accounts Receivable had a debit balance of $60,000 and the Allowance for Uncollectible Accounts had a debit balance of $1,000. If credit losses are estimated at 5% of Accounts Receivable and the estimated method of reporting bad debts is used, then bad debts expense for the year 2016 would be reported as   20.____

    A. $1,000   B. $2,000   C. $3,000   D. $4,000

Questions 21-22.

DIRECTIONS: Questions 21 and 22 are to be answered on the basis of the information below.

Accrued salaries payable on $7,500 had not been recorded on December 31, 2015. Office supplies on hand of $2,500 at December 31, 2016 were erroneously treated as expense instead of inventory. Neither of these errors was discovered or corrected.

21. These two errors would cause the income for 2016 to be

   A. understated by $5,000
   B. overstated by $5,000
   C. understated by $10,000
   D. overstated by $10,000

22. The effect of these errors on the retained earnings at December 31, 2016 would be

   A. understated by $2,500
   B. overstated by $2,500
   C. understated by $5,000
   D. overstated by $5,000

Questions 23-24.

DIRECTIONS: Questions 23 and 24 are to be answered on the basis of the information below.

Arnold, Berg, and Cole operate a retail store under the trade name of ABC. Their partnership agreement provides for equally sharing profits and losses after salaries of $5,000 to Arnold, $10,000 to Berg, and $15,000 to Cole.

23. If the net income of the partnership (prior to salaries to partners) is $21,000, then Arnold's share of the profits, considering all aspects of the agreement, is determined to be

   A. $2,000   B. $3,000   C. $5,000   D. $7,000

24. The share of the profits that apply to Berg, similarly, is determined to be

   A. $2,000   B. $3,000   C. $5,000   D. $7,000

Questions 25-27.

DIRECTIONS: Questions 25 through 27 are to be answered on the basis of the following information.

The Kay Company currently uses FIFO for inventory valuation. Their records for the year ended June 30, 2017 reflect the following:

   July 1, 2016 inventory   100,000 units @ $7.50
   Purchases during year   400,000 units @ $8.00
   Sales during year   350,000 units @ $15.00
   Expenses exclusive of income taxes $1,290,000
   Cash balance on June 30, 2016 $250,000
   Income tax rate   45%

Assume the July 1, 2016 inventory will be the LIFO base inventory.

25. If the company should change to the LIFO as of June 30, 2017, then their income before taxes for the year ended June 30, 2017, as compared with the income FIFO method, will be

   A. *increased* by $50,000
   B. *decreased* by $50,000
   C. *increased* by $100,000
   D. *decreased* by $100,000

26. Assuming the given tax rate (45%), the use of the LIFO method will result in an approximate tax expense for fiscal 2017 of

   A. $45,000   B. $50,000   C. $72,000   D. $94,500

27. Assuming the given tax rate (45%), the use of the LIFO inventory method, compared with the FIFO method, will result in a change in the approximate income tax expense for fiscal 2017 as follows:

   A. *increase* of $22,500
   B. *decrease* of $22,500
   C. *increase* of $45,000
   D. *decrease* of $45,000

28. An accountant in an agency, in addition to his regular duties, has been assigned to train you, a newly appointed assistant accountant. He is not giving you the training you believe you need in order to perform your duties. Accordingly, the most appropriate first step that you, an assistant accountant, should take in order to secure the needed training is to

   A. register for the appropriate courses at the local college as soon as possible
   B. advise the accountant in a formal memo that his apparent lack of interest in your training is impeding your progress
   C. discuss the matter with the accountant privately and try to discover what seems to be the problem
   D. secure such training informally from more sympathetic accountants in the agency

29. You, an assistant accountant, have worked very hard and successfully helped complete a difficult audit of a large corporation doing business in the city. Your supervisor gives you a brief nod of approval when you expected a more substantial degree of recognition. You are angry and feel unappreciated.
   Of the following, the most appropriate course of action for you to take would be to

   A. voice your displeasure to your fellow workers at being taken for granted by an unappreciative supervisor
   B. say nothing now and assume that your supervisor's nod of approval may be his customary acknowledgement of efforts well done
   C. let your supervisor know that he owes you something by repeatedly stressing the outstanding job you've done
   D. ease off on your work quality and productivity until your efforts are finally appreciated

30. You, an assistant accountant, have been assisting in an audit of the books and records of businesses as a member of a team. The accountant in charge of your group tells you to start preliminary work independently on a new audit. This audit is to take place at the offices of the business. The business officers have been duly notified of the audit date. Upon arrival at their offices, you find that their records and files are in disarray and that their personnel are antagonistic and uncooperative. Of the following, the MOST desirable action for you to take is to

    A. advise the business officers that serious consequences may follow unless immediate cooperation is secured
    B. accept whatever may be shown or told you on the grounds that it would be unwise to further antagonize uncooperative personnel
    C. inform your supervisor of the situation and request instructions
    D. leave immediately and return later in the expectation of encountering a more cooperative attitude

30. ___

KEY (CORRECT ANSWERS)

1. A	11. C	21. C
2. B	12. D	22. A
3. D	13. B	23. A
4. D	14. B	24. D
5. B	15. A	25. B
6. C	16. B	26. C
7. A	17. B	27. B
8. A	18. D	28. C
9. C	19. C	29. B
10. B	20. D	30. C

EXAMINATION SECTION
TEST 1

DIRECTIONS: Each question or incomplete statement is followed by several suggested answers or completions. Select the one that BEST answers the question or completes the statement. *PRINT THE LETTER OF THE CORRECT ANSWER IN THE SPACE AT THE RIGHT.*

1. The independent auditor's PRIMARY objective in reviewing internal control is to provide
   A. assurance of the client's operational efficiency
   B. a basis for reliance on the system and determination of the scope of the auditing procedures
   C. a basis for suggestions for improving the client's accounting system
   D. evidence of the client's adherence to prescribed managerial policies

   1.____

2. If there is an increase in work-in-process inventory during a period,
   A. cost of goods sold will be greater than cost of goods manufactured
   B. cost of goods manufactured will be greater than cost of goods sold
   C. manufacturing costs (production costs) for the period will be greater than cost of goods manufactured
   D. manufacturing costs for the period will be less than cost of goods manufactured

   2.____

Questions 3-4.

DIRECTIONS: Questions 3 and 4 are to be answered on the basis of the information given below about the Parr Company and the Farr Company.

The Parr Company purchased 800 of the 1,000 outstanding shares of the Farr Company's common stock for $80,000 on January 1, 2021. During 2021, the Farr Company declared dividends of $8,000 and reported earnings for the year of $20,000.

3. Using the equity method, the investment in Farr Company on the Parr Company's books should show a balance, at December 31, 2021, of
   A. $89,600   B. $$86,400   C. $80,000   D. $73,600

   3.____

4. If, instead of using the equity method, the Parr Company uses the cost method, the balance, at December 31, 2021, in the investment account, should be
   A. $96,000   B. $86,400   C. $80,000   D. $73,600

   4.____

Questions 5-6.

DIRECTIONS: Questions 5 and 6 are to be answered on the basis of the information given below about the Fame Corporation.

The Fame Corporation has 50,000 shares of $10 par value common stock authorized, issued, and outstanding. The 50,000 shares were issued at $12 per share. The retained earnings of the company are $60,000.

5. Assuming that the Fame Corporation reacquired 1,000 of its common shares at $15 per share and the par value method of accounting for treasury stock was used, the result would be that
   A. stockholders' equity would increase by $15,000
   B. capital in excess of par would decrease by at least $2,000
   C. retained earnings would decrease by $5,000
   D. common stock would decrease by at least $15,000

6. Assuming that the Fame Corporation reissued 1,000 of its common shares at $11 per share and the cost method of accounting for treasury stock was used, the result would be that
   A. book value per share of common stock would decrease
   B. retained earnings would decrease by $11,000
   C. donated surplus would be credited for $5,500
   D. a gain on reissue of treasury stock account would be charged

7. On January 31, 2012, when the Montana Corporation's stock was selling at $36 per share, its capital accounts were as follows:
   Capital Stock (par value $20; 100,000 shares issued) $2,000,000
   Premium on Capital Stock   800,000
   Retained Earnings   4,550,000
   If the corporation declares a 100% stock dividend and the par value per share remains at $20, the value of the capital stock would
   A. remain the same
   B. increase to $5,600,000
   C. increase to $5,000,000
   D. decrease

8. In a conventional form of the statement of sources and application of funds, which one of the following would NOT be included?
   A. Periodic amortization of premium of bonds payable
   B. Machinery, fully depreciated and scrapped
   C. Patents written off
   D. Treasury stock purchased from a stockholder

Questions 9-11.

DIRECTIONS: Questions 9 through 11 are to be answered on the basis of the balance sheet shown below for the Argo, Baron and Schooster partnership.

Cash	$ 20,000
Other assets	180,000
Total	$200,000
Liabilities	$50,000
Argo Capital (40%)	37,000
Baron Capital (40%)	65,000
Schooster Capital (20%)	48,000
Total	$200,000

9. If George is to be admitted as a new 1/6 partner without recording goodwill or bonus, George should contribute cash of
   A. $40,000   B. $36,000   C. $33,333   D. $30,000

9.____

10. Assume that Schooster is paid $51,000 by George for his interest in the partnership.
Which of the following choices shows the CORRECT revised capital account for each partner?
   A. Argo, $38,500; Baron, $66,500; George, $51,000
   B. Argo, $38,500; Baron, $66,500; George, $48,000
   C. Argo, $37,000; Baron, $65,000; George, $51,000
   D. Argo, $37,000; Baron, $65,000; George, $48,000

10.____

11. Assume that George had not been admitted as a partner but that the partnership was dissolved and liquidated on the basis of the original balance sheet. Non-cash assets with a book value of $90,000 were sold for $50,000 cash. After payment of creditors, all available cash was distributed.
Which of the following choices MOST NEARLY shows what each of the partners would receive?
   A. Argo, $0; Baron, $13,333; Schooster, $6,667
   B. Argo, $0; Baron, $3,000; Schooster, $17,000
   C. Argo, $6,667; Baron, $6,667; Schooster, $6,666
   D. Argo, $8,000; Baron, $8,000; Schooster, $4,000

11.____

12. Which one of the following should be restricted to ONLY one employee in order to assure proper control of assets?
   A. Access to safe deposit box
   B. Placing orders and maintaining relationship with a principal vendor
   C. Collection of a particular past due account
   D. Custody of the petty cash fund

12.____

13. To assure proper internal control, the quantities of materials ordered may be omitted from that copy of the purchase order which is
    A. sent to the accounting department
    B. retained in the purchasing department
    C. sent to the party requisitioning the material
    D. sent to the receiving department

14. The Amey Corporation has an inventory of raw materials and parts made up of many different items which are of small value individually but of significant total value
    A BASIC control requirement in such a situation is that
    A. perpetual inventory records should be maintained for all items
    B. physical inventories should be taken on a cyclical basis rather than at year end
    C. storekeeping, production, and inventory record-keeping functions should be separated
    D. requisitions for materials should be approved by a corporate officer

15. In conducting an audit of plant assets, which of the following accounts MUST be examined in order to ascertain that additions to plant assets have been correctly stated and reflect charges that are properly capitalized?
    A. Accounts Receivable
    B. Sales Income
    C. Maintenance and Repairs
    D. Investments

16. Which one of the following is a control procedure that would prevent a vendor's invoice from being paid twice (once upon the original invoice and once upon the monthly statement?
    A. Attaching the receiving report to the disbursement support papers
    B. Prenumbering of disbursement vouchers
    C. Using a limit of reasonable test
    D. Prenumbering of receiving reports

17. A "cut-off" bank statement is received for the period December 1 to December 10, 2021. Very few of the checks listed on the November 30, 2021 bank reconciliation cleared during the cut-off period.
    Of the following, the MOST likely reason for this is
    A. kiting
    B. using certified checks rather than ordinary checks
    C. holding the cash disbursement book open after year end
    D. overstating year-end bank balance

18. "Lapping" is a common type of defalcation.
    Of the audit techniques listed below, the one MOST effective in the detection of "lapping" is
    A. reconciliation of year-end bank statements
    B. review of duplicate deposit slips
    C. securing confirmations from banks
    D. checking footings in cash journals

19. Of the following, the MOST common argument against the use of the negative accounts receivable confirmation is that
    A. cost per response is excessively high
    B. statistical sampling techniques cannot be applied to selection of the sample
    C. client's customers may assume that the confirmation is a request for payment
    D. lack of response does not necessarily indicate agreement with the balance

Questions 20-21.

DIRECTIONS   Questions 20 and 21 are to be answered on the basis of the information in the Payroll Summary given below. This Payroll Summary represents payroll for a monthly period for a particular agency.

		PAYROLL SUMMARY				
		Deductions				
Employee	Total Earnings	FICA	Withhold Tax	State Tax	Other	Net Pay
W	450.00	26.00	67.00	18.00	6.00	333.00
X	235.00	14.00	33.00	8.00	2.00	178.00
Y	341.00	20.00	52.00	14.00	5.00	250.00
Z	275.00	16.00	30.00	6.00	2.40	220.60
Totals	1,301.00	76.00	182.00	46.00	15.40	981.60

20. Based on the data given above, the amount of cash that would have to be available to pay the employees on payday is
    A. $1,301.00   B. $981.60   C. $905.60   D. $662.60

21. Based on the data given above, the amount of cash that would have to be governmental depository is
    A. $334.00   B. $182.00   C. $158.00   D. $76.00

Questions 22-23.

DIRECTIONS: Questions 22 and 23 are to be answered on the basis of the information given below concerning an imprest fund.

Assume a $1,020 imprest fund for cash expenditures is maintained in your agency. As an audit procedure, the fund is counted and the following information results from that count.

Unreimbursed bills properly authorized	$ 345.00
Check from employee T. Jones	125.00
Check from Supervisor R. Riggles	250.00
I.O.U. signed by employee J. Sloan	100.00
Cash counted—coins and bills	200.00
TOTAL	$1,020.00

22. A PROPER statement of cash on hand based upon the data shown above should show a balance of
    A. $1,020   B. $1,000   C. $545   D. $200

23. Based upon the data shown above, the account reflects IMPROPER handling of the fund because
    A. vouchers are unreimbursed
    B. the cash balance is too low
    C. employees have used it for loans and check-cashing purposes
    D. the unreimbursed bills should not have been authorized

Question 24-25.

DIRECTIONS: Questions 24 and 25 are to be answered on the basis of the following information.

The following information was taken from the ledgers of the Past Present Corporation:

Common stock had been issued for $6,000,000. This represents 400,000 shares of stock at a stated value of $5 per share. Fifty-thousand shares are in the treasury. These 50,000 shares were acquired for $25 per share. The total undistributed net income since the origin of the corporation was $3,750,000 as of December 31, 2021. Ten-thousand of the treasury stock shares were sold in January 2022 for $30 per share.

24. Based only on the information given above, the TOTAL stockholders' equity that should have been shown on the balance sheet as of December 31, 2021 was
    A. $2,000,000   B. $6,000,000   C. $8,500,000   D. $9,750,000

25. Based only on the information given above, the Retained Earnings as of December 31, 2022 will be
    A. $2,000,000   B. $3,750,000   C. $3,800,000   D. $4,050,000

Questions 26-29.

DIRECTIONS: Questions 26 through 29 are to be answered on the basis of the following information.

A statement of income for the Dartmouth Corporation for the 2022 fiscal year follows:

Sales	$89,000	
Cost of Goods Sold	20,000	
Gross Margin		$34,000
Expenses		20,000
Net Income Before Income Taxes		$14,000
Provision for Income Taxes (50%)		7,000
Net Income		$7,000

The following errors were discovered relating to the 2022 fiscal year:
- Closing inventory was overstated by $2,100
- A $3,000 expenditure was capitalized during fiscal year 2022 that should have been listed under Expenses. This was subject to 10% amortization taken for a full year
- Sales included $3,500 of deposits received from customers for future orders.
- Accrued salaries of $850 were not included in Cost of Goods Sold
- Interest receivable of $500 was omitted

Assume that the books were not closed and that you have prepared a corrected income statement. Answer Questions 26 through 29 on the basis of your corrected income statement.

26. The gross margin after accounting for adjustments SHOULD BE
    A. $37,500   B. $35,400   C. $31,900   D. $27,550

27. The adjusted income before income taxes SHOULD BE
    A. $5,350   B. $9,550   C. $15,000   D. $15,850

28. The adjusted income after provision for a 50% tax rate SHOULD BE
    A. $7,925   B. $7,500   C. $4,500   D. $2,675

29. After making adjustments, sales to be reported for fiscal year 2022 SHOULD BE
    A. unchanged
    B. increased by $3,500
    C. decreased by $3,500
    D. reduced by $2,100

Questions 30-33.

DIRECTIONS: Questions 30 through 33 are to be answered on the basis of the following budget for the Utility Corporation for 2022.

Sales	$550,000
Cost of Goods Sold	320,000
Selling Expenses	75,000
General Expenses	60,000
Net Income	95,000

30. If sales are actually 12% above the budget, then ACTUAL sales will be
    A. $550,000   B. $562,000   C. $605,000   D. $616,000

31. If actual costs of goods sold exceed the budget by 10%, then the cost of goods sold will be
    A. $294,400   B. $320,000   C. $605,000   D. $352,000

32. If selling expenses exceed the budget by 10%, the INCREASE in the selling expenses will be
    A. $750   B. $3,750   C. $7,500   D. $8,333

33. If general expenses are under budget by 5%, they will amount to 33.____
    A. $3,000   B. $57,000   C. $60,000   D. $63,000

Questions 34-35.

DIRECTIONS: Questions 34 and 35 are to be answered on the basis of the following information.

The Yontiff Company began business on January 2, 2021. During the first month, credit sales totaled $100,000. During February, credit sales totaled $125,000. 70% of credit sales are paid during the month of sale, and the balance is collected during the following month.

34. During the month of January, cash collections on credit sales totaled 34.____
    A. $70,000   B. $95,000   C. $100,000   D. $125,000

35. During the month of February, cash collections on credit sales totaled 35.____
    A. $70,000   B. $87,500   C. $117,505   D. $125,000

Questions 36-38.

DIRECTIONS: Questions 36 through 38 are to be answered on the basis of the following information taken from the balance sheet of the F Corporation.

        Common Stock $200 Par $1,400,000
        Premium on Common Stock   115,000
        Deficit   50,000

36. The number of shares of common stock outstanding is 36.____
    A. 200   B. 700   C. 7,000   D. 14,000

37. The total equity is 37.____
    A. $50,000   B. $115,000   C. $1,400,000   D. $1,465,000

38. The book value per share of stock is MOST NEARLY 38.____
    A. $160   B. $200   C. $209   D. $312

Questions 39-40.

DIRECTIONS: Questions 39 and 40 are to be answered on the basis of the following statement.

You are examining the expense accounts of a contractor and you discover that, although his payroll records show proper deductions from employees, he has never provided for the payroll tax expenses for these employees.

39. As a result of the oversight described in the above statement, the Costs of 39.____
    Construction in Progress as given on the balance sheet will be _____ on the balance sheet.
    A. understated   B. overstated   C. unaffected   D. omitted

40. As a result of the oversight described in the above statement, the balance sheet for the firm will reflect an
    A. overstatement of liabilities
    B. understatement of liabilities
    C. overstatement of assets
    D. understatement of assets

40.____

KEY (CORRECT ANSWERS)

1.	B	11.	D	21.	A	31.	D
2.	C	12.	D	22.	D	32.	C
3.	A	13.	D	23.	C	33.	B
4.	C	14.	C	24.	C	34.	A
5.	B	15.	C	25.	B	35.	C
6.	A	16.	A	26.	D	36.	C
7.	A	17.	C	27.	A	37.	D
8.	B	18.	B	28.	D	38.	C
9.	D	19.	D	29.	C	39.	A
10.	D	20.	B	30.	D	40.	B

TEST 2

DIRECTIONS: Each question or incomplete statement is followed by several suggested answers or completions. Select the one that BEST answers the question or completes the statement. *PRINT THE LETTER OF THE CORRECT ANSWER IN THE SPACE AT THE RIGHT.*

Questions 1-4.

DIRECTIONS: Questions 1 through 4 are to be answered on the basis of the following information.

In the audit of the Audell Co. for the calendar year 2021, the accountant noted the following errors.

- An adjusting entry for $10 for interest accrued on a customer's $4,000, 60-day, 6% note was not recorded at the end of December 2020. In 2021, the total interest received was credited to interest income.
- Equipment was leased on December 31, 2020 and rental of $300 was paid in advance for the next three months and charged to Rent Expense.
- On November 1, 2020, space was rented at $75 per month. The tenant paid six months rent in advance which was credited to Rent Income.
- Salary expenses in the amount of $60 were not recorded at the end of 2020
- Depreciation in the amount of $80 was not recorded at the end of 2020.
- An error of $200 in addition on the year-end 2020 physical inventory sheets was made. The inventory was overstated.

1. The amount of the net adjustment to Net Income for 2020 is 1.____
   A. Credit $430   B. Debit $430   C. Credit $600   D. Credit $560

2. The net change in asset values at December 31, 2020 is 2.____
   A. Credit $70   B. Debit $70   C. Debit $110   D. Credit $60

3. The net change in liabilities at December 31, 2020 is 3.____
   A. Debit $360   B. Credit $430   C. Debit $560   D. Credit $360

4. The net change in Owner's Equity at December 31, 2020 is 4.____
   A. Debit $720   B. Debit $430   C. Credit $320   D. Credit $720

5. As of October 2, 2021, the Mallory Company's books reflect a balance of $2,104.75 in its account entitled Cash in Bank. A comparison of the book entries with the bank statement showed the following: 5.____
   - A check in the amount of $76.25 outstanding at the end of September 2021 had not been returned.
   - One check, which was returned with the October bank statement, in the amount of $247 had been recorded in the October cash book as $274.
   - A total of $139 of checks issued in October had not been returned with the October bank statement.
   - A deposit of $65 was returned by the bank because of insufficient funds.

68

- The bank charged a service charge of $3.25 for the month of October which as not reported on the books until November.
- The bank had credited $247 representing a note collected in the amount of $250 which was not picked up on the books until November.
- A deposit of $305.50 was recorded on the books in October but not on the bank statement.

The balance in the bank as shown on the bank statement at October 31, 2021 is
   A. $2,220.25   B. $2,104.75   C. $2,006.25   D. $2,315.25

Questions 6-8.

DIRECTIONS: Questions 6 through 8 are to be answered on the basis of the following information.

    A company purchased three cars at $3,150 each on April 2, 2021. Depreciation is to be computed on a mileage basis. The estimated mileage to be considered is 50,000 miles, with a trade-in value of $650 for each car.
    After having been driven 8,400 miles, car #1 was completely destroyed on November 23, 2020 and not replaced. The insurance company paid $2,500 for the loss.
    As of December 31, 2020, of the two remaining cars, car #2 had been driven 10,300 miles and car #3 was driven 11,500 miles.
    On July 10, 2021, after having been driven a total of 24,600 miles, car #2 was sold for $1,800.
    Car #3, after having been driven a total of 27,800 miles, was traded in on December 28, 2021 for a new car (#4) that had a list price of $3,000. On the purchase of car #4, the dealer allowed a trade-in value of $1,850.

6.   The balance in the Allowance for Depreciation account at December 31, 2020 is
    A. $1,850   B. $910   C. $1,090   D. $1,110

7.   The depreciation expense for the calendar year 2021 is
    A. $1,530   B. $2,000   C. $2,500   D. $3,00

8.   The book value of the new car (car #4) using the income tax method is
    A. $1,850   B. $3,000   C. $2,500   D. $2,910

Questions 9-10.

DIRECTIONS: Questions 9 and 10 are to be answered on the basis of the following information.

    The Pneumatic Corp. showed the following balance sheets at December 31, 2020 and December 31, 2021

	12/31/2020	12/31/2021
Cash	$6,700	$9,000
Accounts Receivable	12,000	11,500
Merchandise Inventory	31,500	32,000
Prepaid Expenses	800	1,000
Equipment	21,000	28,000
	$72,000	$81,500
Accumulated Depreciation	$4,000	$5,500
Accounts Payable	17,500	11,500
Common Stock - $5 Per Share	10,000	5,000
Premium on Common Stock	40,000	50,000
Retained Earnings	10,500	13,000
	$72,000	$81,500

Additional Information:
A further examination of the Pneumatic Corp.'s transactions for 2021 showed the following:
- Depreciation on equipment, $2,500]
- Fully depreciated equipment that cost $1,000 was scrapped, and cost and related accumulated depreciation eliminated.
- Two thousand shares of common stock were sold at $6 per share.
- A cash dividend of $10,000 was paid.

9. A statement of funds provided and applied for the calendar year 2021 would show that net income provided funds in the amount of
    A. $2,500   B. $9,500   C. $15,000   D. $22,500

10. The funds applied to the acquisition of equipment during the calendar year 2021 amounts to
    A. $21,000   B. $28,000   C. $1,000   D. $8,000

11. A company's Wage Expense account had a $19,100 debit balance before any adjustment at the end of its December 31, 2020 fiscal year. The company employs five individuals who earn $15 per day and were paid on Friday for the five days ending on Friday, December 25, 2020. All employees worked during the week ending January 2, 2021.
    The adjusted balance in the Wage Expense account at December 31, 2020 is
    A. $22,300   B. $19,100   C. $19,250   D. $19,325

Questions 12-13.

DIRECTIONS: Questions 12 and 13 are to be answered on the basis of the following information.

4 (#2)

The Peach Corp.'s books reflect an account entitled "Allowance for Bad Debts" showing a credit balance of $1,510 as of January 1, 2020.

During 2020, it wrote off 735 of bad debts and increased the allowance for bad debts by an amount equal to ¼ of 1% of sales of $408,000.

During 2021, it wrote off $605 as bad debts and recorded $50 of a debt that had been previously written off.

An addition to the "Allowance for Bad Debts" was provided based upon ¼ of 1% on $478,000 of sales.

12. The balance in the "Allowance for Bad Debts" account at December 31, 2021 is   12._____
    A. $2,550   B. $2,434   C. $2,360   D. $2,240

13. The amount of the Bad Debt expense for the calendar year 2021 is   13._____
    A. $1,195   B. $1,405   C. $2,000   D. $1,510

14. The following ratio is based upon the 2021 financial statements of the Chino Corp.:   14._____

    Number of Times Bond Interest Earned: $28,000/$3,000 = 9.33 times

    Information relating to the corrections of the income data for 2021 follows:
- Rental payment for December 2021 at $2,00 per month had been recorded in January 2022. No provision has been made for this expense on the 2021 books.
- During 2021, merchandise shipped on consignment and unsold had been recorded as
    Debit – Accounts Receivable $4,000
    Credit – Sales   4,000

(Note: The inventory of this merchandise was properly recorded.)

If the described ratio, Number of Times Bond Interest Earned, was recomputed, taking into consideration the corrections listed above and ignoring tax factors in the calculations, the recomputed <u>Number of Times Bond Interest Earned</u> would be _____ times.
    A. 8.10   B. 7.60   C. 6.20   D. 5.10

Questions 15-16.

DIRECTIONS: Questions 15 and 16 are to be answered on the basis of the following information.

The Delancey Department Store, Inc. sells merchandise on the installment basis. The selling price of its merchandise is $500 and its cost is $325.

At the end of its fiscal year, an examination of its accounts showed the following:

Sales (Installment	$500,000
Installment Accounts Receivable	280,000
Sales Commissions	15,000
Other Expenses	32,000

15. The net income for the fiscal year, before taxes, using the installment method 15.____
    of reporting income, is
    A. $30,000   B. $20,000   C. $15,000   D. $35,000

16. The balance in the Deferred Income Account at the end of the fiscal year is 16.____
    A. $110,000   B. $80,000   C. $76,000   D. $98,000

Questions 17-18.

DIRECTIONS: Questions 17 and 18 are to be answered on the basis of the following information.

The Merrimac Company sold 8,800 units of a product at $5 per unit during the calendar year 2021. In addition, it has the following transactions:

	Units	Unit Cost
Inventory – January 1, 2021	1,000	$2.80
Purchases – March	1,000	3.00
June	4,000	3.20
September	3,000	3.30
October	1,000	3.50

17. If we assume that selling and administrative expenses cost $8,800, the Net 17.____
    Income for the calendar year 2021, using the first-in first-out method of costing
    inventory is
    A. $8,460   B. $7,360   C. $6,600   D. $4,070

18. If we assume that selling and administrative expenses cost $8,800, the Net 18.____
    Income for the calendar year 2021, using the last-in first-out method of costing
    inventory, is
    A. $4,550   B. $7,360   C. $6,600   D. $5,000

19. L. Eron and A. Pilott are partners who share income and losses in the ratio 19.____
    3:2, respectively. The balance in the Profit and Loss account on December 31,
    2021, prior to distribution to the partners, is $20,800. Before distributing any
    profits to the partnership in the agreed ratio, L. Eron is to be given credit for
    interest on his loan of $60,000, outstanding for the entire year, at 6% per
    annum. A. Pilott is to receive a bonus of 10% of the net income over $5,100,
    after deducting the bonus to himself and the interest to L. Eron.
    Giving consideration to all the above information, the total amount of net
    income to be credited to A. Pilott is
    A. $8,320   B. $2,080   C. $7,540   D. $15,700

Questions 20-21.

DIRECTIONS: Questions 20 and 21 are to be answered on the basis of the following information.

6 (#2)

Schneider and Samuels are partners with capital balances on December 31, 2021 of $15,000 and $25,000, respectively. They share profits in a ratio of 2:1.

Goroff is to be admitted to the partnership. He agrees to be admitted as a partner with a cash investment to give him a one-third interest in the capital and profits of the business. All the parties agree that the goodwill to be granted to Goroff should be valued at $6,000.

20. The required cash to cover Goroff's investment in a business partnership according to the terms stated is
    A. $20,000   B. $14,000   C. $6,000   D. $25,000

21. After his cash investment, and all other initial entries, the credit to Goroff's Capital account is
    A. $20,000   B. $14,000   C. $6,000   D. $25,000

22. The Marlin Corp. sold 7,800 units of its product at $25 per unit and suffered a net loss for its calendar year ending December 31, 2021 of $2,000. The fixed expenses amounted to $80,000 and the variable expenses $117,000. The Marlin Corp. believes that by expending $20,000 in an advertising campaign, it could increase its sales, retaining the $25 per unit selling price, to generate a profit.
    Assuming the above facts, the sales revenue for 2021 reflecting the break-even point is
    A. $195,000   B. $217,000   C. $250,000   D. $300,000

23. The Anide Corp., which keeps its books on the accrual basis, had the following transactions for its calendar year ending December 31, 2021.
    - April 15, 2021 – Authorized the issuance of $3,000,000 of 5.5%, 20 year bonds, dated May 1, 2021. Interest to be paid November 1 and May 1.
    - June 1, 2021 – Sold the entire issue at $2,965,150 plus accrued interest
    - November 1, 2021 – Paid the interest due.
    The interest expense for the calendar year 2021 is
    A. $85,000   B. $165,000   C. $110,000   D. $97,300

Questions 24-26.

DIRECTIONS: Questions 24 through 26 are to be answered on the basis of the following information.

The following information was taken from a worksheet that was used in the preparation of the balance sheet and the profit and loss statement of the Hott Company for 2021.

7 (#2)

The Balance Sheet Contained	Amount
Travel Expense Unpaid	$995
Legal and Collection Fees – Prepaid in Advance	672
Interest Received in Advance	469

The Profit and Loss Statement Contained	Amount
Travel Expenses	$7,343
Legal and Collection Fees	5,461
Interest Income	3,114

The proper adjusting and closing entries were made on the books of the company by the accountant and the described information was reported on the financial statements. The books are kept on an accrual basis.

On the basis of the above facts, the balance in each of the following accounts in the trial balance, before adjusting and closing entries were made, was as follows:

24. Travel Expense Account
    A. $8,338   B. $7,343   C. $6,348   D. $995

25. Legal and Collection Fees Account
    A. $672   B. $4,789   C. $5,461   D. $6,133

26. Interest Income Account
    A. $3,583   B. $3,114   C. $2,645   D. $469

Questions 27-28.

DIRECTIONS: Questions 27 and 28 are to be answered on the basis of the following information

The following is the stockholder's equity section of a corporation:
Preferred Stock (7%, cumulative, non-participating, $100 par value
, 5,000 shares issued and outstanding) $500.000

Common Stock ($1.00 par value, 500,000, issued and outstanding)   500,000
                                                                        $1,000,000

Deficit   (40,000)
                                                                         $960,000

27. Assuming two years' dividends in arrears on the preferred stock, the book value per share of common stock is
    A. 78¢   B. 80¢   C. 63¢   D. 94¢

28. Assuming two years' dividends in arrears on the preferred stock, the book value per share of preferred stock is
    A. $130   B. $114   C. $98   D. $140

Questions 29-30.

DIRECTIONS: Questions 29 and 30 are to be answered on the basis of the following information.

Regina Corporation on December 31, 2021 had the following stockholder's equity:

Common Stock ($10 par value), 10,000 shares authorized and outstanding)	$100,000
Retained Earnings	20,000
	$120,000

On December 31, 2021, the Astro Corp. purchased 9,000 shares of the Regina Corporation's outstanding shares, paying $14 per share

29. The entry to eliminate Astro Corp.'s investment and the Regina Corporation's stockholder's equity on consolidation would show a debit or credit to an account called "Excess of Cost Over Book Value" of
    A. Credit, $18,000
    B. Debit, $18,000
    C. Debit, $15,000
    D. Debit, $19,000

30. If the Regina Corporation had earnings for the calendar year 2021 of $10,000 and had paid out $8,000 of these earnings as dividends, and an entry to eliminate the Astro Corp.'s investment and the Regina Corporation's stockholder's equity were made, the minority stockholder's equity would be
    A. $15,000   B. $10,100   C. $12,200   D. $14,800

KEY (CORRECT ANSWERS)

1.	B	11.	D	21.	A
2.	A	12.	B	22.	C
3.	D	13.	A	23.	D
4.	B	14.	B	24.	C
5.	A	15.	A	25.	D
6.	C	16.	D	26.	A
7.	A	17.	B	27.	A
8.	D	18.	C	28.	B
9.	C	19.	C	29.	B
10.	D	20.	B	30.	C

TEST 3

DIRECTIONS: Each question or incomplete statement is followed by several suggested answers or completions. Select the one that BEST answers the question or completes the statement. *PRINT THE LETTER OF THE CORRECT ANSWER IN THE SPACE AT THE RIGHT.*

1. For the measurement of net income to be as realistic as possible, it is DESIRABLE that revenue be recognized at the point that
    A. cash is collected from customers
    B. an order for merchandise or services is received from a customer
    C. a deposit or advance payment is received from a customer
    D. goods are delivered or services are rendered to customers

    1._____

2. An accounting principle must receive substantial authoritative support to qualify as "generally accepted."
   Many organizations and agencies have been influential in the development of generally accepted accounting principles, but the MOST influential leadership has come from the
    A. New York Stock Exchange
    B. American Institute of Certified Public Accountants
    C. Securities and Exchange Commission
    D. American Accounting Association

    2._____

3. In which one of the following ways does the declaration and payment of a cash dividend affect corporate net income? It _____ net income.
    A. does not affect   B. reduces
    C. increases   D. capitalizes

    3._____

4. Under which one of the following headings of the corporate balance sheet should the liability for a dividend payable in stock appear?
    A. Current Liabilities   B. Long Term Liabilities
    C. Stockholders' Equity   D. Current Assets

    4._____

5. In which one of the following is "Working Capital" MOST likely to be found?
    A. Income Statement
    B. Analysis of Retained Earnings
    C. Computation of Cost of Capital
    D. Statement of Funds Provided and Applied

    5._____

6. Which one of the following procedures is NOT generally mandatory in auditing a merchandising corporation?
    A. Physical observation of inventory count
    B. Written circularization of accounts receivable
    C. Confirmation of bank balance
    D. Circularization of the stockholders

    6._____

76

7. A company purchased office supplies during 2021 in the total amount of $1,400 and charged the entire amount to the asset account. An inventory of supplies taken on December 31, 2021 shows the cost of unused supplies to be $250. The entry to record this fact, assuming the books have not been closed, involves
   A. credit to capital
   B. debit to supplies Expense
   C. credit to supplies expense
   D. debit to supplies on hand

7.____

8. A corporation's records show $600,000 (credit) in net sales, $200,000 (debit) in year-end accounts receivable, and $2,000 (debit) in Allowance for Bad Debts. The company's aged schedule of accounts receivable indicates a probable future loss from failure to collect year-end receivables in the amount of $6,000.
   Of the following, the MOST correct entry to adjust the Allowance for Bad Debts at year-end is
   A. $1,000 credit
   B. $4,000 credit
   C. $8,000 debit
   D. $8,000 credit

8.____

Questions 9-10.

DIRECTIONS: Questions 9 and 10 are to be answered on the basis of the following information.

A company commenced business in 2021 and purchased inventory as follows:

March	100 units @	$5	$500
June	300	6	1,800
October	200	7	1,400
November	500	6	3,500
December	100	6	600
TOTAL	1,200		$7,800

**Units sold in 2021 amounted to 1,200

9. Under the LIFO inventory principle, the value of the remaining inventory is
   A. $1,700   B. $1,875   C. $2,145   D. $2,225

9.____

10. Under the FIFO inventory principle, the value of the remaining inventory is
    A. $1,650   B. $1,875   C. $2,000   D. $2,025

10.____

11. When doing a trial balance, assume that, as a result of a single error, the total of the credit balances is greater than the total of the debit balances. Which one of the following single errors could NOT be the cause of this discrepancy?
    A. Failure to post a debit
    B. Posting a debit as a credit
    C. Failure to post a credit
    D. Posting a credit twice

11.____

Questions 12-13.

DIRECTIONS: Questions 12 and 13 are to be answered on the basis of the following information.

A and B are partners with capital balances of $20,000 and $30,000, respectively, at June 30, 2021, who share profits and losses, 40% and 60%, respectively. On July 1, 2021, C is to be admitted into the partnership under the following conditions:
- Partnership assets are to be revalued and increased by $10,000
- C is to invest $40,000 but be credited for $30,000 while the remaining $10,000 is to be credited to A and B to compensate them for their pre-existing goodwill.

12. After C is admitted and the proper entries are made, A's capital account will have a credit balance of
    A. $24,500   B. $28,000   C. $30,200   D. $36,000

13. After the admission of C to the partnership, C's share of profits and losses is agreed upon at 20%.
    Assuming no other adjustments, the new percentage for profit and loss distribution to A will be
    A. 18%   B. 32%   C. 36%   D. 45%

14. A company reports as income for tax purposes $70,000 and its book income before the provision for income taxes is $100,000.
    Assuming a 50% tax rate, the PROPER tax expense to be recorded following tax allocation procedures is
    A. $33,000   B. $40,000   C. $50,000   D. $60,000

15. The relationship between the total of cash and current receivables to total current liabilities is commonly referred to by accountants as the
    A. acid-test ratio   B. cross-statement ratio
    C. current ratio   D. R.O.I. ratio

16. On a statement of sources and application of funds, the depreciation expense is normally shown as a(n)
    A. addition to operating income   B. subtraction from funds provided
    C. addition to funds applied   D. reduction from operating income

17. Company A owns 100% of the capital stock of Company B and reports on a consolidated basis. During the year, Company A sold inventory to Company B at a profit of $100,000. One-half of this inventory has been sold at year-end by Company B to the public.
    Which one of the following would be the MOST correct adjustment, if any, to make the consolidated retained earnings conform to generally accepted accounting principles?
    A. Decrease by $50,000   B. Increase by $50,000
    C. Increase by $100,000   D. No adjustment

18. X, Y, and Z are partners with capital of $11,000, $12,000, and $4,500. X has a loan due from the partnership to him of $2,000. Profits and losses are shared in the ratio of 4:5:1, respectively. The partnership has paid off all outside liabilities, and its remaining assets consist of $9,000 in cash and $20,500 of accounts receivable. The partners agree to disburse the $9,000 to themselves in such a way that, even if one of the receivables is realized, no partner will have been overpaid.
Under these conditions, which of the following MOST NEARLY represents the amount to be paid to partner X?
    A. $1,960   B. $3,200   C. $4,800   D. $5,000

19. R Company needs $2,000,000 to finance an expansion of plant facilities. The company expects to earn a return of 15% on this investment before considering the cost of capital or income taxes. The average income tax rate for the R Company is 40%.
If the company raises the funds by issuing 6% bonds at face value, the earnings available to common stockholders after the new plant facilities are in operation may be expected to increase by
    A. $65,000   B. $70,000   C. $108,000   D. $116,000

20. The budget for a given factory overhead cost was $150,000 for the year. The actual cost for the year was $125,000.
Based on these facts, it can be said that the plant manager has done a better job than expected in controlling this cost if the cost is a
    A. semi-variable cost
    B. variable cost and actual production was 83 1/3% of budgeted production
    C. semi-variable cost which includes a fixed element of $25,000 per period
    D. variable cost and actual production was equal to budgeted production

21. The Home Office account on the books of the City Branch shows a credit balance of $15,000 at the end of a year and the City Branch account on the books of the Home Office shows a debit balance of $12,000.
Of the following, the MOST likely reason for the discrepancy in the two accounts is that
    A. merchandise shipped by the Home Office to the branch has not been recorded by the branch
    B. the Home Office has not recorded a branch loss for the first quarter of the year
    C. the branch has just mailed a check for $3,000 to the Home Office which has not yet been received by the Home Office
    D. the Home Office has not yet recorded the branch profit for the first quarter of the year

22. The concept of matching costs and revenues means that
    A. the expenses offset against revenues should be related to the same time period
    B. revenues are at least as great as expenses on the average
    C. revenues and expenses are equal
    D. net income equals revenues minus expenses for the same earning period

23. If the inventory at the end of the current year is understated, and the error is not caught during the following year, the effect is to
    A. *overstate* the income for the two-year period
    B. *overstate* income this year and *understate* income next year
    C. *understate* income this year and *overstate* income next year
    D. *understate* income this year, with no effect on the income of the next year

23.____

KEY (CORRECT ANSWERS)

1.	D		11.	C
2.	B		12.	B
3.	A		13.	B
4.	C		14.	C
5.	D		15.	A
6.	D		16.	A
7.	B		17.	A
8.	D		18.	C
9.	A		19.	C
10.	C		20.	D

21.	D
22.	A
23.	C

INTERPRETING STATISTICAL DATA
GRAPHS, CHARTS AND TABLES
EXAMINATION SECTION
TEST 1

DIRECTIONS: Each questioner incomplete statement is followed by several suggested answers or completions. Select the one that BEST answers the question or completes the statement. *PRINT THE LETTER OF THE CORRECT ANSWER IN THE SPACE AT THE RIGHT.*

Questions 1-3.

DIRECTIONS: Questions 1 through 3 are to be answered SOLELY on the basis of the following table.

QUARTERLY SALES REPORTED BY MAJOR INDUSTRY GROUPS

DECEMBER 2021 – FEBRUARY 2023
Reported Sales, Taxable & Non-Taxable (in Millions)

Industry Groups	12/21-2/22	3/22-5/22	6/22-8/22	9/22-11/22	12/22-2/23
Retailers	2,802	2,711	2,475	2,793	2,974
Wholesalers	2,404	2,237	2,269	2,485	2,974
Manufacturers	3,016	2,888	3,001	3,518	3,293
Services	1,034	1,065	984	1,132	1,092

1. The trend in total reported sales may be described as

    A. downward
    B. downward and upward
    C. horizontal
    D. upward

2. The two industry groups that reveal a similar seasonal pattern for the period December 2021 through November 2022 are

    A. retailers and manufacturers
    B. retailers and wholesalers
    C. wholesalers and manufacturers
    D. wholesalers and service

3. Reported sales were at a MINIMUM between

    A. December 2021 and February 2022
    B. March 2022 and May 2022
    C. June 2022 and August 2022
    D. September 2022 and November 2022

TEST 2

DIRECTIONS: Each question or incomplete statement is followed by several suggested answers or completions. Select the one that BEST answers the question or completes the statement. *PRINT THE LETTER OF THE CORRECT ANSWER IN THE SPACE AT THE RIGHT*

Questions 1-4.

DIRECTIONS: Questions 1 through 4 are to be answered SOLELY on the basis of the following information.

The income elasticity of demand for selected items of consumer demand in the United States are:

Item	Elasticity
Airline Travel	5.66
Alcohol	.62
Dentist Fees	1.00
Electric Utilities	3.00
Gasoline	1.29
Intercity Bus	1.89
Local Bus	1.41
Restaurant Meals	.75

1. The demand for the item listed below that would be MOST adversely affected by a decrease in income is

   A. alcohol
   B. electric utilities
   C. gasoline
   D. restaurant meals

2. The item whose relative change in demand would be the same as the relative change in income would be

   A. dentist fees
   B. gasoline
   C. restaurant meals
   D. none of the above

3. If income increases by 12 percent, the demand for restaurant meals may be expected to increase by

   A. 9 percent
   B. 12 percent
   C. 16 percent
   D. none of the above

4. On the basis of the above information, the item whose demand would be MOST adversely affected by an increase in the sales tax from 7 percent to 8 percent to be passed on to the consumer in the form of higher prices

   A. would be airline travel
   B. would be alcohol
   C. would be gasoline
   D. cannot be determined

TEST 3

DIRECTIONS: Each question or incomplete statement is followed by several suggested answers or completions. Select the one that BEST answers the question or completes the statement. *PRINT THE LETTER OF THE CORRECT ANSWER IN THE SPACE AT THE RIGHT.*

Questions 1-3.

DIRECTIONS: Questions 1 through 3 are to be answered SOLELY on the basis of the following graphs depicting various relationships in a single retail store.

GRAPH 1
RELATIONSHIP BETWEEN NUMBER OF CUSTOMERS STORE AND TIME OF DAY

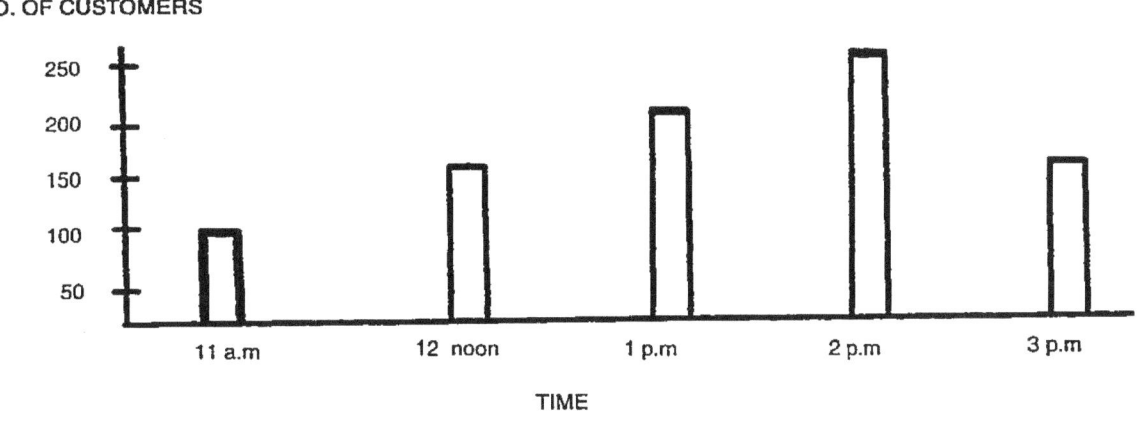

GRAPH II
RELATIONSHIP BETWEEN NUMBER OF CHECK-OUT LANES AVAILABLE IN STORE AND WAIT TIME FOR CHECK-OUT

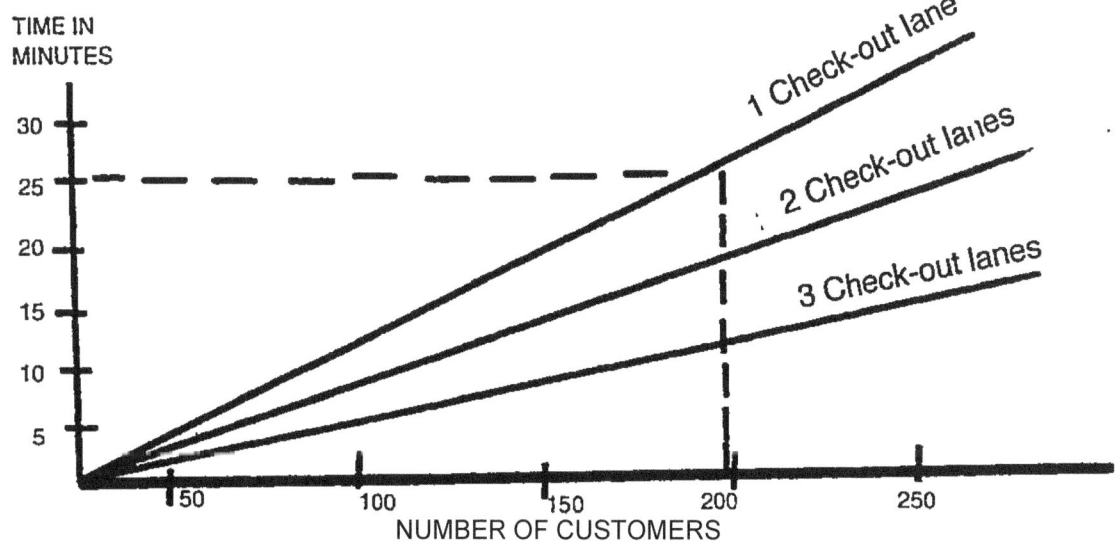

Note the dotted lines in Graph II. They demonstrate that, if there are 200 people in the store and only one check-out lane is open, the wait time will be 25 minutes.

83

1. At what time would a person be most likely NOT to have to wait more than 15 minutes if only one check-out lane is open?

   A. 11 A.M.   B. 12 Noon   C. 1 P.M.   D. 3 P.M.

2. At what time of day would a person have to wait the LONGEST to check out if three check-out lanes are available?

   A. 11 A.M.   B. 12 Noon   C. 1 P.M.   D. 2 P.M

3. The difference in wait times between 1 and 3 check-out lanes at 3 P.M. is MOST NEARLY

   A. 5   B. 10   C. 15   D. 20

TEST 4

DIRECTIONS: Each question or incomplete statement is followed by several suggested answers or completions. Select the one that BEST answers the question or completes the statement. *PRINT THE LETTER OF THE CORRECT ANSWER IN THE SPACE AT THE RIGHT.*

Questions 1-4.

DIRECTIONS: Questions 1 through 4 are to be answered SOLELY on the basis of the graph below.

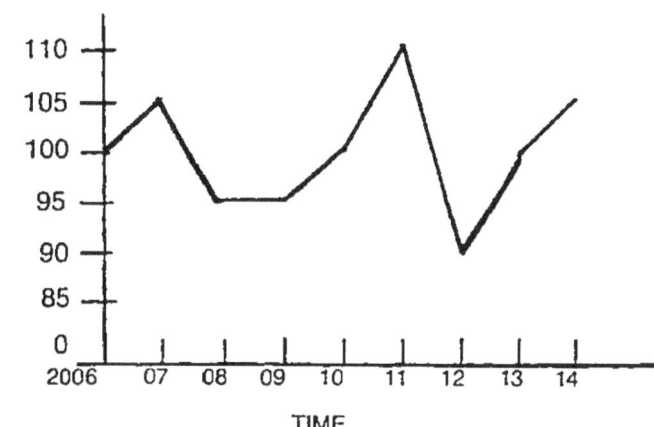

1. Of the following, during what four-year period did the average output of computer operators fall BELOW 100 sheets per hour?

   A. 2007-10   B. 2008-11   C. 2010-13   D. 2011-14

2. The average percentage change in output over the previous year's output for the years 2009 to 2012 is MOST NEARLY

   A. 2   B. 0   C. -5   D. -7

3. The difference between the actual output for 2012 and the projected figure based upon the average increase from 2006-2011 is MOST NEARLY

   A. 18   B. 20   C. 22   D. 24

4. Assume that after constructing the above graph you, an analyst, discovered that the average number of entries per sheet in 2012 was 25 (instead of 20) because of the complex nature of the work performed during that period.
   The average output in sheets per hour for the period 2010-13, expressed in terms of 20 items per sheet, would then be MOST NEARLY

   A. 95   B. 100   C. 105   D. 110

TEST 6

DIRECTIONS: Each question or incomplete statement is followed by several suggested answers or completions. Select the one that BEST answers the question or completes the statement. *PRINT THE LETTER OF THE CORRECT ANSWER IN THE SPACE AT THE RIGHT.*

Questions 1-3.

DIRECTIONS: Questions 1 through 3 are to be answered on the basis of the following data assembled for a cost-benefit analysis.

	Cost	Benefit
No program	0	0
Alternative W	$ 3,000	$ 6,000
Alternative X	$10,000	$17,000
Alternative Y	$17,000	$25,000
Alternative Z	$30,000	$32,000

1. From the point of view of selecting the alternative with the best cost benefit ratio, the BEST alternative is Alternative

   A. W   B. X   C. Y   D. Z

2. From the point of view of selecting the alternative with the best measure of net benefit, the BEST alternative is Alternative

   A. W   B. X   C. Y   D. Z

3. From the point of view of pushing public expenditure to the point where marginal benefit equals or exceeds marginal cost, the BEST alternative is Alternative

   A. W   B. X   C. Y   D. Z

TEST 6

DIRECTIONS: Each question or incomplete statement is followed by several suggested answers or completions. Select the one that BEST answers the question or completes the statement. *PRINT THE LETTER OF THE CORRECT ANSWER IN THE SPACE AT THE RIGHT.*

Questions 1-3.

DIRECTIONS: Questions 1 through 3 are to be answered SOLELY on the basis of the following data.

A series of cost-benefit studies of various alternative health programs yields the following results:

Program	Benefit	Cost
K	30	15
L	60	60
M	300	150
N	600	500

In answering Questions 1 and 2, assume that all programs can be increased or decreased in scale without affecting their individual benefit-to-cost ratios.

1. The benefit-to-cost ratio of Program M is

   A. 10:1   B. 5:1   C. 2:1   D. 1:2

2. The budget ceiling for one or more of the programs included in the study is set at 75 units. It may MOST logically be concluded that

   A. Programs K and L should be chosen to fit within the budget ceiling
   B. Program K would be the most desirable one that could be afforded
   C. Program M should be chosen rather than Program K
   D. the choice should be between Programs M and K

3. If no assumptions can be made regarding the effects of change of scale, the MOST logical conclusion, on the basis of the data available, is that

   A. more data are needed for a budget choice of program
   B. Program K is the most preferable because of its low cost and good benefit-to-cost ratio
   C. Program M is the most preferable because of its high benefits and good benefit-to-cost ratio
   D. there is no difference between Programs K and M, and either can be chosen for any purpose

TEST 7

DIRECTIONS: Each question or incomplete statement is followed by several suggested answers or completions. Select the one that BEST answers the question or completes the statement. *PRINT THE LETTER OF THE CORRECT ANSWER IN THE SPACE AT THE RIGHT.*

Questions 1-6.

DIRECTIONS: Questions 1 through 6 are to be answered SOLELY on the basis of the information contained in the charts below which relate to the budget allocations of City X, a small suburban community. The charts depict the annual budget allocations by Department and by expenditures over a five-year period.

CITY X BUDGET IN MILLIONS OF DOLLARS
TABLE I. Budget Allocations by Department

Department	2017	2018	2019	2020	2021
Public Safety	30	45	50	40	50
Health and Welfare	50	75	90	60	70
Engineering	5	8	10	5	8
Human Resources	10	12	20	10	22
Conservation & Environment	10	15	20	20	15
Education & Development	15	25	35	15	15
TOTAL BUDGET	120	180	225	150	180

TABLE II. Budget Allocations by Expenditures

Category	2017	2018	2019	2020	2021
Raw Materials & Machinery	36	63	68	30	98
Capital Outlay	12	27	56	15	18
Personal Services	72	90	101	105	64
TOTAL BUDGET	120	180	225	150	180

1. The year in which the SMALLEST percentage of the total annual budget was allocated to the Department of Education and Development is

   A. 2017   B. 2018   C. 2020   D. 2021

2. Assume that in 2020 the Department of Conservation and Environment divided its annual budget into the three categories of expenditures and in exactly the same proportion as the budget shown in Table II for the year 2020. The amount allocated for capital outlay in the Department of Conservation and Environment's 2020 budget was MOST NEARLY _____ million.

   A. $2   B. $4   C. $6   D. $10

3. From the year 2018 to the year 2020, the sum of the annual budgets for the Departments of Public Safety and Engineering showed an overall _____ million.

   A. decline; SB
   B. increase; $7
   C. decline; S15
   D. increase; S22

4. The LARGEST dollar increase in departmental budget allocations from one year to the next was in _____ from _____.

   A. Public Safety; 2017 to 2018
   B. Health and Welfare; 2017 to 2018
   C. Education and Development; 2019 to 2020
   D. Human Resources; 2019 to 2020

5. During the five-year period, the annual budget of the Department of Human Resources was GREATER than the annual budget for the Department of Conservation and Environment in _____ of the years.

   A. none   B. one   C. two   D. three

6. If the total City X budget increases at the same rate from 2021 to 2022 as it did from 2020 to 2021, the total City X budget for 2022 will be MOST NEARLY _____ million.

   A. $180   B. $200   C. $210   D. $215

TEST 8

DIRECTIONS: Each question or incomplete statement is followed by several suggested answers or completions. Select the one that BEST answers the question or completes the statement. *PRINT THE LETTER OF THE CORRECT ANSWER IN THE SPACE AT THE RIGHT.*

Questions 1-3.

DIRECTIONS: Questions 1 through 3 are to be answered SOLELY on the basis of the following information.

Assume that in order to encourage Program A, the State and Federal governments have agreed to make the following reimbursements for money spent on Program A, provided the unreimbursed balance is paid from City funds.

During Fiscal Year 2021-2022 - For the first $2 million expended, 50% Federal reimbursement and 30% State reimbursement; for the next $3 million, 40% Federal reimbursement and 20% State reimbursement; for the next $5 million, 20% Federal reimbursement and 10% State reimbursement. Above $10 million expended, no Federal or State reimbursement.

During Fiscal Year 2022-2023 - For the first $1 million expended, 30% Federal reimbursement and 20% State reimbursement; for the next $4 million, 15% Federal reimbursement and 10% State reimbursement. Above $5 million expended, no Federal or State reimbursement.

1. Assume that the Program A expenditures are such that the State reimbursement for Fiscal Year 2021-2022 will be $1 million.
   Then, the Federal reimbursement for Fiscal Year 2021-2022 will be

   A. $1,600,000 B. $1,800,000
   C. $2,000,000 D. $2,600,000

2. Assume that $8 million were to be spent on Program A in Fiscal Year 2022-2023.
   The TOTAL amount of unreimbursed City funds required would be

   A. $3,500,000 B. $4,500,000
   C. $5,500,000 D. $6,500,000

3. Assume that the City desires to have a combined total of $6 million spent in Program A during both the Fiscal Year 2021-2022 and the Fiscal Year 2022-2023.
   Of the following expenditure combinations, the one which results in the GREATEST reimbursement of City funds is _____ in Fiscal Year 2021-2022 and _____ in Fiscal Year 2022-2023.

   A. $5 million; $1 million   B. $4 million; $2 million
   C. $3 million; $3 million   D. $2 million; $4 million

KEY (CORRECT ANSWERS)

TEST 1

1. D
2. C
3. C

TEST 2

1. B
2. A
3. A
4. D

TEST 3

1. A
2. D
3. B

TEST 4

1. A
2. B
3. C
4. C

TEST 5

1. A
2. C
3. C

TEST 6

1. C
2. D
3. A

TEST 7

1. D
2. A
3. A
4. B
5. B
6. D

TEST 8

1. B
2. D
3. A

READING COMPREHENSION
UNDERSTANDING AND INTERPRETING WRITTEN MATERIAL
EXAMINATION SECTION
TEST 1

DIRECTIONS: Each question or incomplete statement is followed by several suggested answers or completions. Select the one that BEST answers the question or completes the statement. *PRINT THE LETTER OF THE CORRECT ANSWER IN THE SPACE AT THE RIGHT.*

Questions 1-3.

DIRECTIONS: Questions 1 through 3 are to be answered SOLELY on the basis of the following passage.

Every organization needs a systematic method of checking its operations as a means to increase efficiency and promote economy. Many successful private firms have instituted a system of audit or internal inspections to accomplish these ends. Law enforcement organizations, which have an extremely important service to *sell*, should be no less zealous in developing efficiency and economy in their operations. Periodic, organized, and systematic inspections are one means of promoting the achievement of these objectives. The necessity of an organized inspection system is perhaps greatest in those law enforcement groups which have grown to such a size that the principal officer can no longer personally supervise or be cognizant of every action taken. Smooth and effective operation demands that the head of the organization have at hand some tool with which he can study and enforce general policies and procedure and also direct compliance with day-to-day orders, most of which are put into execution outside his sight and hearing. A good inspection system can serve as that tool.

1. The central thought of the above passage is that a system of inspections within a police department
    A. is unnecessary for a department in which the principal officer can personally supervise all official actions taken
    B. should be instituted at the first indication that there is any deterioration in job performance by the force
    C. should be decentralized and administered by first-line supervisory officers
    D. is an important aid to the police administrator in the accomplishment of law enforcement objectives

1._____

2. The MOST accurate of the following statements concerning the need for an organized inspection system in a law enforcement organization is: It is
    A. never needed in an organization of small size where the principal officer can give personal supervision
    B. most needed where the size of the organization prevents direct supervision by the principal officer
    C. more needed in law enforcement organizations than in private firms
    D. especially needed in an organization about to embark upon a needed expansion of services

2._____

3. According to the above passage, the head of the police organization utilizes the internal inspection system
   A. as a tool which must be constantly re-examined in the light of changing demands for police service
   B. as an administrative technique to increase efficiency and promote economy
   C. by personally visiting those areas of police operation which are outside his sight and hearing
   D. to augment the control of local commanders over detailed field operations

Questions 4-10.

DIRECTIONS: Questions 4 through 10 are to be answered SOLELY on the basis of the following passage.

Job evaluation and job rating systems are intended to introduce scientific procedures. Any type of approach, when properly used, will give satisfactory results. The Point System, when properly validated by actual use, is more likely to be suitable for general use than the ranking system. In many aspects, the Factor Comparison Plan is a point system tied to money values. Of course, there may be another system that combines the ranking system with the point system, especially during the initial stages of the development of the program. After the program has been in use for some time, the tendency is to drop off the ranking phase and continue the use of the point system.

In the ranking system of rating of jobs, every job within the plant is arranged in some order, either from the one with the simplest qualifications to the one with maximum requirements, or in the reverse order. This system should be preceded by careful job analysis and the writing of accurate job descriptions before the rating process is undertaken. It is possible, of course, to take the jobs as they are found in the business enterprise and use the names as they are without any attempt at standardization, and merely rank them according to the general overall impression of the raters. Such a procedure is certain to fall short of what may reasonably be expected of job rating. Another procedure that is in reality merely a modification of the simple rating described above is to establish a series of grades or zones and arrange all he jobs in the plant into groups within these grades and zones. The practice in most common use is to arrange all the jobs in the plant according to their requirements by rating them and then to establish the classification or groups.

The actual ranking of jobs may be done by one individual, several individuals, or a committee. If several individuals are working independently on the task, it will usually be found that, in general, they agree but that their rankings vary in certain details. A conference between the individuals, with each person giving his reasons why he rated one way or another, usually produces agreement. The detailed job descriptions are particularly helpful when there is disagreement among raters as to the rating of certain jobs. It is not only possible but desirable to have workers participate in the construction of the job description and in rating the job.

4. The MAIN theme of this passage is
   A. the elimination of bias in job rating
   B. the rating of jobs by the ranking system
   C. the need or accuracy in allocating points in the point system
   D. pitfalls to avoid in selecting key jobs in the Factor Comparison Plan

5. The ranking system of rating jobs consists MAINLY of
   A. attaching a point value to each ratable factor of each job prior to establishing an equitable pay scale
   B. arranging every job in the organization in descending order and then following this up with a job analysis of the key jobs
   C. preparing accurate job descriptions after a job analysis and then arranging all jobs either in ascending or descending order based on job requirements
   D. arbitrarily establishing a hierarchy of job classes and grades and then fitting each job into a specific class and grade based on the opinions of unit supervisors

6. The above passage states that the system of classifying jobs MOST used in an organization is to
   A. organize all jobs in the organization in accordance with their requirements and then create categories or clusters of jobs
   B. classify all jobs in the organization according to the titles and rank by which they are currently known in the organization
   C. establish a pre-arranged series of grades or zones and then fit all jobs into one of the grades or zones
   D. determine the salary currently being paid for each job and then rank the jobs in order according to salary

7. According to the above passage, experience has shown that when a group of raters is assigned to the job evaluation task and each individual rates independently of the others, the raters GENERALLY
   A. *agree* with respect to all aspects of their rankings
   B. *disagree* with respect to all or nearly all aspects of the rankings
   C. *disagree* on overall ratings, but agree on specific rating factors
   D. *agree* on overall rankings, but have some variance in some details

8. The above passage states that the use of a detailed job description is of special value when
   A. employees of an organization have participated in the preliminary step involved in actual preparation of the job description
   B. labor representatives are not participating in ranking of the jobs
   C. an individual rater who is unsure of himself is ranking the jobs
   D. a group of raters is having difficulty reaching unanimity with respect to ranking a certain job

9. A comparison of the various rating systems as described in the above passage shows that
   A. the ranking system is not as appropriate for general use as a properly validated point system
   B. the point system is the same as the Factor Comparison Plan except that it places greater emphasis on money

C. no system is capable of combining the point system and the Factor Comparison Plan
D. the point system will be discontinued last when used in combination with the Factor comparison System

10. The above passage implies that the PRINCIPAL reason for creating job evaluation and rating systems was to help
    A. overcome union opposition to existing salary plans
    B. base wage determination on a more objective and orderly foundation
    C. eliminate personal bias on the part of the trained scientific job evaluators
    D. management determine if it was overpricing the various jobs in the organizational hierarchy

Questions 11-13.

DIRECTIONS: Questions 11 through 13 are to be answered SOLELY on the basis of the following passage.

The common sense character of the merit system seems so natural to most Americans that many people wonder why it should ever have been inoperative. After all, the American economic system, the most phenomenal the world has ever known, is also founded on a rugged selective process which emphasizes the personal qualities of capacity, industriousness, and productivity. The criteria may not have always been appropriate and competition has not always been fair, but competition there was, and the responsibilities and the rewards—with exceptions, of course—have gone to those who could measure up in terms of intelligence, knowledge, or perseverance. This has been true not only in the economic area, in the money-making process, but also in achievement in the professions and other walks of life.

11. According to the above passage, economic rewards in the United State have
    A. always been based on appropriate, fair criteria
    B. only recently been based on a competitive system
    C. not going to people who compete too ruggedly
    D. usually gone to those people with intelligence, knowledge, and perseverance

12. According to the above passage, a merit system is
    A. an unfair criterion on which to base rewards
    B. unnatural to anyone who is not American
    C. based only on common sense
    D. based on the same principles as the American economic system

13. According to the above passage, it is MOST accurate to say that
    A. the United States has always had a civil service merit system
    B. civil service employees are very rugged
    C. the American economic system has always been based on a merit objective
    D. competition is unique to the American way of life

Questions 14-15.

DIRECTIONS: Questions 14 and 15 are to be answered SOLELY on the basis of the following passage.

In-basket tests are often used to assess managerial potential. The exercise consists of a set of papers that would be likely to be found in the in-basket of an administrator or manager at any given time, and requires the individuals participating in the examination to indicate how they would dispose of each item found in the in-basket. In order to handle the in-basket effectively, they must successfully manage their time, refer and assign some work to subordinates, juggle potentially conflicting appointments and meetings, and arrange for follow-up of problems generated by the items in the in-basket. In other words, the in-basket test is attempting to evaluate the participants' abilities to organize their work, set priorities, delegate, control, and make decisions.

14. According to the above passage, to succeed in an in-basket test, an administrator must
    A. be able to read very quickly
    B. have a great deal of technical knowledge
    C. know when to delegate work
    D. arrange a lot of appointments and meetings

14._____

15. According to the above passage, all of the following abilities are indications of managerial potential EXCEPT the ability to
    A. organize and control
    B. manage time
    C. write effective reports
    D. make appropriate decisions

15._____

Questions 16-19.

DIRECTIONS: Questions 16 through 19 are to be answered SOLELY on the basis of the following passage.

A personnel researcher has at his disposal various approaches for obtaining information, analyzing it, and arriving at conclusions that have value in predicting and affecting the behavior of people at work. The type of method to be used depends on such factors as the nature of the research problem, the available data, and the attitudes of those people being studied to the various kinds of approaches. While the experimental approach, with its use of control groups, is the most refined type of study, there are others that are often found useful in personnel research. Surveys, in which the researcher obtains facts on a problem from a variety of sources, are employed in research on wages, fringe benefits, and labor relations. Historical studies are used to trace the development of problems in order to understand them better and to isolate possible causative factors. Case studies are generally developed to explore all the details of a particular problem that is representative of other similar problems. A researcher chooses the most appropriate form of study for the problem he is investigating. He should recognize, however, that the experimental method, commonly referred to as the scientific method, if used validly and reliably, gives the most conclusive results.

16. The above passage discusses several approaches used to obtain information on particular problems.
Which of the following may be MOST reasonably concluded from the passage? A(n)
    A. historical study cannot determine causative factors
    B. survey is often used in research on fringe benefits
    C. case study is usually used to explore a problem that is unique and unrelated to other problems
    D. experimental study is used when the scientific approach to a problem fails

16._____

17. According to the above passage, all of the following are factors that may determine the type of approach a researcher uses EXCEPT
    A. the attitudes of people toward being used in control groups
    B. the number of available sources
    C. his desire to isolate possible causative factors
    D. the degree of accuracy he requires

17._____

18. The words *scientific method*, as used in the last sentence of the above passage, refer to a type of study which, according to the above passage
    A. uses a variety of sources
    B. traces the development of problems
    C. uses control groups
    D. analyzes the details of a representative problem

18._____

19. Which of the following can be MOST reasonably concluded from the above passage?
In obtaining and analyzing information on a particular problem, a researcher employs the method which is the
    A. most accurate
    B. most suitable
    C. least expensive
    D. least time-consuming

19._____

Questions 20-25.

DIRECTIONS: Questions 20 through 25 are to be answered SOLELY on the basis of the following passage.

The quality of the voice of a worker is an important factor in conveying to clients and co-workers his attitude and, to some degree, his character. The human voice, when not consciously disguised, may reflect a person's mood, temper, and personality. It has been shown in several experiments that certain character traits can be assessed with better than chance accuracy through listening to the voice of an unknown person who cannot be seen.
Since one of the objectives of the worker is to put clients at ease and to present an encouraging and comfortable atmosphere, a harsh, shrill, or loud voice could have a negative effect. A client who displays emotions of anger or resentment would probably be provoked even further by a caustic tone. In a face-to-face situation, an unpleasant voice may be compensated for, to some degree, by a concerned and kind facial expression. However, when one speaks on the telephone, the expression on one's face cannot be seen by the listener. A supervising clerk who wishes to represent himself effectively to clients should try to eliminate as many faults as possible in striving to develop desirable voice qualities.

7 (#1)

20. If a worker uses a sarcastic tone while interviewing a resentful client, the client, according to the above passage, would MOST likely
    A. avoid the face-to-face problem
    B. be ashamed of his behavior
    C. become more resentful
    D. be provoked to violence

    20.____

21. According to the passage, experiments comparing voice and character traits have demonstrated that
    A. prospects for improving an unpleasant voice through training are better than chance
    B. the voice can be altered to project many different psychological characteristics
    C. the quality of the human voice reveals more about the speaker than his words do
    D. the speaker's voice tells the hearer something about the speaker's personality

    21.____

22. Which of the following, according to the above passage, is a person's voice MOST likely to reveal?
    His
    A. prejudices
    B. intelligence
    C. social awareness
    D. temperament

    22.____

23. It may be MOST reasonably concluded from the above passage that an interested and sympathetic expression on the face of a worker
    A. may induce a client to feel certain he will receive welfare benefits
    B. will eliminate the need for pleasant vocal qualities in the interviewer
    C. may help to make up for an unpleasant voice in the interviewer
    D. is desirable as the interviewer speaks on the telephone to a client

    23.____

24. Of the following, the MOST reasonable implication of the above paragraph is that a worker should, when speaking to a client, control and use his voice to
    A. simulate a feeling of interest in the problems of the client
    B. express his emotions directly and adequately
    C. help produce in the client a sense of comfort and security
    D. reflect his own true personality

    24.____

25. It may be concluded from the above passage that the PARTICULAR reason for a worker to pay special attention to modulating her voice when talking on the phone to a client is that, during a telephone conversation
    A. there is a necessity to compensate for the way in which a telephone distorts the voice
    B. the voice of the worker is a reflection of her mood and character
    C. the client can react only on the basis of the voice and words she hears
    D. the client may have difficulty getting a clear understanding over the telephone

    25.____

KEY (CORRECT ANSWERS)

1.	D	11.	D
2.	B	12.	D
3.	B	13.	C
4.	B	14.	C
5.	C	15.	C
6.	A	16.	B
7.	D	17.	D
8.	D	18.	C
9.	A	19.	B
10.	B	20.	C

21. D
22. D
23. C
24. C
25. C

TEST 2

DIRECTIONS: Each question or incomplete statement is followed by several suggested answers or completions. Select the one that BEST answers the question or completes the statement. *PRINT THE LETTER OF THE CORRECT ANSWER IN THE SPACE AT THE RIGHT.*

Questions 1-3.

DIRECTIONS: Questions 1 through 3 are to be answered SOLELY on the basis of the following paragraph.

Suppose you are given the job of printing, collating, and stapling 8,000 copies of a ten-page booklet as soon as possible. You have available one photo-offset machine, a collator with an automatic stapler, and the personnel to operate these machines. All will be available for however long the job takes to complete. The photo-offset machine prints 5,000 impressions an hour, and it takes about 15 minutes to set up a plate. The collator, including time for insertion of pages and stapling, can process about 2,000 booklets an hour. (Answers should be based on the assumption that there are no breakdowns or delays.)

1. Assuming that all the printing is finished before the collating is started, if the job is given to you late Monday and your section can begin work the next day and is able to devote seven hours a day, Monday through Friday, to the job until it is finished, what is the BEST estimate of when the job will be finished?
    A. Wednesday afternoon of the same week
    B. Thursday morning of the same week
    C. Friday morning of the same week
    D. Monday morning of the next week

1.____

2. An operator suggests to you that instead of completing all the printing and then beginning collating and stapling, you first print all the pages for 4,000 booklets, so that they can be collated and stapled while the last 4,000 pages are being printed.
    If you accepted this suggestion, the job would be completed
    A. sooner but would require more man-hours
    B at the same time using either method
    C. later and would require more man-hours
    D. sooner but there would be more wear and tear on the plates

2.____

3. Assume that you have the same assignment and equipment as described above, but 16,000 copies of the booklet are needed instead of 8,000.
    If you decided to print 8,000 complete booklets, then collate and staple them while you started printing the next 8,000 booklets, which of the following statements would MOST accurately describe the relationship between this new method and your original method of printing all the booklets at one time, and then collating and stapling them? The
    A. job would be completed at the same time regardless of the method used
    B. new method would result in the job's being completed 3½ hours earlier
    C. original method would result in the job's being completed an hour later
    D. new method would result in the job's being completed 1½ hours earlier

3.____

Questions 4-6.

DIRECTIONS: Questions 4 through 6 are to be answered SOLELY on the basis of the following passage.

When using words like company, association, council, committee, and board in place of the full official name, the writer should not capitalize these short forms unless he intends them to invoke the full force of the institution's authority. In legal contracts, in minutes, or in formal correspondence where one is speaking formally and officially on behalf of the company, the term Company is usually capitalized, but in ordinary usage, where it is not essential to load the short form with this significance, capitalization would be excessive. (Example: The company will have many good openings for graduates this June.)

The treatment recommended for short forms of place names is essentially the same as that recommended for short forms of organizational names. In general, we capitalize the full form but not the short form. If Park Avenue is referred to in one sentence, then the *avenue* is sufficient in subsequent references. The same is true with words like building, hotel, station, and airport, which are capitalized when part of a proper name changed (Pan Am Building, Hotel Plaza, Union Station, O'Hare Airport), but are simply lower-cased when replacing these specific names.

4. The above passage states that USUALLY the short forms of names of organizations
   A. and places should not be capitalized
   B. and places should be capitalized
   C. should not be capitalized, but the short forms of names of places should be capitalized
   D. should be capitalized, but the short forms of names of places should not be capitalized

4.____

5. The above passage states that in legal contracts, in minutes, and in formal correspondence, the short forms of names of organizations should
   A. usually not be capitalized   B. usually be capitalized
   C. usually not be used   D. never be used

5.____

6. It can be inferred from the above passage that decisions regarding when to capitalize certain words
   A. should be left to the discretion of the writer
   B. should be based on generally accepted rules
   C. depend on the total number of words capitalized
   D. are of minor importance

6.____

Questions 7-10.

DIRECTIONS: Questions 7 through 10 are to be answered SOLELY on the basis of the following passage.

Use of the systems and procedures approach to office management is revolutionizing the supervision of office work. This approach views an enterprise as an entity which seeks to fulfill definite objectives. Systems and procedures help to organize repetitive work into a routine, thus reducing the amount of decision making required for its accomplishment. As a result, employees are guided in their efforts and perform only necessary work. Supervisors are relieved of any details of execution and are free to attend to more important work. Establishing work guides which require that identical tasks be performed the same way each time permits standardization of forms, machine operations, work methods, and controls. This approach also reduces the probability of errors. Any error committed is usually discovered quickly because the incorrect work does not meet the requirement of the work guides. Errors are also reduced through work specialization, which allows each employee to become thoroughly proficient in a particular type of work. Such proficiency also tends to improve the morale of the employees.

7. The above passage states that the accuracy of an employee's work is INCREASED by
   A. using the work specialization approach
   B. employing a probability sample
   C. requiring him to shift at one time into different types of tasks
   D. having his supervisor check each detail of work execution

8. Of the following, which one BEST expresses the main theme of the above passage? The
   A. advantages and disadvantages of the systems and procedures approach to office management
   B. effectiveness of the systems and procedures approach to office management in developing skills
   C. systems and procedures approach to office management as it relates to office costs
   D. advantages of the systems and procedures approach to office management for supervisors and office workers

9. Work guides are LEAST likely to be used when
   A. standardized forms are used
   B. a particular office task is distinct and different from all others
   C. identical tasks are to be performed in identical ways
   D. similar work methods are expected from each employee

10. According to the above passage, when an employee makes a work error, it USUALLY
    A. is quickly corrected by the supervisor
    B. necessitates a change in the work guides
    C. can be detected quickly if work guides are in use
    D. increases the probability of further errors by that employee

Questions 11-12.

DIRECTIONS: Questions 11 and 12 are to be answered SOLELY on the basis of the following passage.

The coordination of the many activities of a large public agency is absolutely essential. Coordination, as an administrative principle, must be distinguished from and is independent of cooperation. Coordination can be of either the horizontal or the vertical type. In large organizations, the objectives of vertical coordination are achieved by the transmission of orders and statements of policy down through the various levels of authority. It is an accepted generalization that the more authoritarian the organization, the more easily may vertical coordination be accomplished. Horizontal coordination is arrived through staff work, administrative management, and conferences of administrators of equal rank. It is obvious that of the two types of coordination, the vertical kind is more important, for at best horizontal coordination only supplements the coordination effected up and down the line,

11. According to the above passage, the ease with which vertical coordination is achieved in a large agency depends upon
    A. the extent to which control is firmly exercised from above
    B. the objectives that have been established for the agency
    C. the importance attached by employees to the orders and statements of policy transmitted through the agency
    D. the cooperation obtained at the various levels of authority

11.____

12. According to the above passage,
    A. vertical coordination is dependent for its success upon horizontal coordination
    B. one type of coordination may work in opposition to the other
    C. similar methods may be used to achieve both types of coordination
    D. horizontal coordination is at most an addition to vertical coordination

12.____

Questions 13-17.

DIRECTIONS: Questions 13 through 17 are to be answered SOLELY on the basis of the following situation.

Assume that you are a newly appointed supervisor in the same unit in which you have been acting as a provisional for some time. You have in your unit the following workers:

WORKER I: He has always been an efficient worker. In a number of his cases, the clients have recently begun to complain that they cannot manage on the departmental budget.

WORKER II: He has been under selective supervision for some time as an experienced, competent worker. He now begins to be late for his supervisory conferences and to stress how much work he has to do.

WORKER III: He has been making considerable improvement in his ability to handle the details of his job. He now tells you, during an individual conference, that he does not need such close supervision and that he wants to operate more independently. He says that Worker II is always available when he needs a little information or help but, in general, he can manage very well by himself.

5 (#2)

WORKER IV: He brings you a complex case for decision as to eligibility. Discussion of the case brings out the fact that he has failed to consider all the available resources adequately but has stressed the family's needs to include every extra item in the budget. This is the third case of a similar nature that his worker has brought to you recently. This worker and Worker I work in adjacent territory and are rather friendly.

In the following questions, select the option that describes the method of dealing with these workers that illustrate BEST supervisory practice.

13. With respect to supervision of Worker I, the assistant supervisor should 13.____
    A. discuss with the worker, in an individual conference, any problems that he may be having due to the increase in the cost of living
    B. plan a group conference for the unit around budgeting, as both Workers I and IV seem to be having budgetary difficulties
    C. discuss with Workers I and IV together the meaning of money as acceptance or rejection to the clients
    D. discuss with Worker I the budgetary data in each case in relation to each client's situation

14. With respect to supervision of Worker II, the supervisory should 14.____
    A. move slowly with this worker and give him time to learn that the supervisor's official appointment has not changed his attitudes or methods of supervision
    B. discuss the worker's change of attitude and asks him to analyze the reasons for his change in behavior
    C. take time to show the worker how he is avoiding his responsibility in the supervisor-worker relationship and that he is resisting supervision
    D. hold an evaluatory conference with the worker and show him how he is taking over responsibilities that are not his by providing supervision for Worker III

15. With respect to supervision of Worker III, the supervisor should discuss with 15.____
    this worker
    A. why he would rather have supervision from Worker II than from the supervisor
    B. the necessity for further improvement before he can go on selective supervision
    C. an analysis of the improvement that has been made and the extent to which the worker is able to handle the total job for which he is responsible
    D. the responsibility of the supervisor to see that clients receive adequate service

16. With respect to supervision of Worker IV, the supervisor should 16.____
    A. show the worker that resources figures are incomplete but that even if they were complete, the family would probably be eligible for assistance
    B. ask the worker why he is so protective of these families since there are three cases so similar

C. discuss with the worker all three cases at the same time so that the worker may see his own role in the three situations
D. discuss with the worker the reasons for departmental policies and procedures around budgeting

17. With respect to supervision of Workers I and IV, since these two workers are friends and would seem to be influencing each other, the supervisor should 17.____
    A. hold a joint conference with them both, pointing out how they should clear with the supervisor and not make their own rules together
    B. handle the problems of each separately in individual conferences
    C. separate them by transferring one to another territory or another unit
    D. take up the problem of workers asking help of each other rather than from the supervisor in a group meeting

Questions 18-20.

DIRECTIONS: Questions 18 through 20 are to be answered SOLELY on the basis of the following passage.

One of the key supervisory problems in a large municipal recreation department is that many leaders are assigned to isolated playgrounds or small centers, where it is difficult to observe their work regularly. Often their facilities are extremely limited. In such settings, as well as in larger recreation centers, where many recreation leaders tend to have other jobs as well, there tends to be a low level of morale and incentive. Still, it is the supervisor's task to help recreation personnel to develop pride in their work and to maintain a high level of performance. With isolated leaders, the supervisor may give advice or assistance. Leaders may be assigned to different tasks or settings during the year to maximize their productivity and provide new challenges. When it is clear that leaders are no willing to make a real effort to contribute to the department, the possibility of penalties must be considered, within the scope of departmental policy and the union contract. However, the supervisor should be constructive, encourage and assist workers to take a greater interest in their work, be innovative, and try to raise morale and to improve performance in positive ways.

18. The one of the following that would the MOST appropriate title for the above passage is 18.____
    A. Small Community Centers – Pro and Con
    B. Planning Better Recreation Programs
    C. The Supervisor's Task in Upgrading Personnel Performance
    D. The Supervisor and the Municipal Union – Rights and Obligations

19. The above passage makes clear that recreation leadership performance in all recreation playgrounds and centers throughout a large city is 19.____
    A. generally above average, with good morale on the part of most recreation leaders
    B. beyond description since no one has ever observed or evaluated recreation leaders

C. a key test of the personnel department's effort to develop more effective hiring standards
D. of mixed quality, with many recreation leaders having poor morale and a low level of achievement

20. According to the above passage, the supervisor's role is to 20.____
    A. use disciplinary action as his major tool in upgrading performance
    B. tolerate the lack of effort of individual employees since they are assigned to isolated playgrounds or small centers
    C. employ encouragement, advice, and, when appropriate, disciplinary action to improve performance
    D. inform the county supervisor whenever malfeasance or idleness is detected

Questions 21-25.

DIRECTIONS: Questions 21 through 25 are to be answered SOLELY on the basis of the following passage.

EMPLOYEE LEAVE REGULATIONS

Peter Smith, as a full-time permanent city employee under the Career and Salary Plan, earns an *annual leave allowance*. This consists of a certain number of days off a year with pay and may be used for vacation, personal business, and for observing religious holidays. As a newly appointed employee, during his first 8 years of city service, he will earn an annual leave allowance of 20 days off a year (an average of $1^{2}/_{3}$ days off a month). After he has finished 8 full years of working for the city, he will begin earning an additional 5 days off a year. His annual leave allowance, therefore, will then be 25 days a year and will remain at this amount for seven full years. He will begin earning an additional two days off a year at this amount for seven full years. He will begin earning an additional two days off a year after he has completed a total of 15 years of city employment. Therefore, in his sixteenth year of working for the city, Mr. Smith will be earning 27 days off a year as his annual leave allowance (an average of $2¼$ days off a month).

A *sick leave allowance* of one day a month is also given to Mr. Smith, but it can be used only in cases of actual illness. When Mr. Smith returns to work after using sick leave allowance, he must have a doctor's note if the absence is for a total of more than 3 days, but he may also be required to show a doctor's note for absences of 1, 2, or 3 days.

21. According to the above passage, Mr. Smith's annual leave allowance consists 21.____
    of a certain number of days off a year which he
    A. does not get paid for
    B. gets paid for at time and a half
    C. may use for personal business
    D. may not use for observing religious holidays

22. According to the above passage, after Mr. Smith has been working for the city 22.____
    for 9 years, his annual leave allowance will be _____ days a year.
    A. 20   B. 25   C. 27   D. 37

23. According to the above passage, Mr. Smith will begin earning an average of 2 days off a month as his annual leave allowance after he has worked for the city for _____ full years.
    A. 7   B. 8   C. 15   D. 17

24. According to the above passage, Mr. Smith is given a sick leave allowance of
    A. 1 day every 2 months
    B. 1 day per month
    C. $1^{2}/_{3}$ days per month
    D. 2¼ days a month

25. According to the above passage, when he uses sick leave allowance, Mr. Smith may be required to show a doctor's note
    A. even if his absence is for only 1 day
    B. only if his absence is for more than 2 days
    C. only if his absence is for more than 3 days
    D. only if his absence is for 3 days or more

KEY (CORRECT ANSWERS)

1.	C	11.	A
2.	C	12.	D
3.	D	13.	D
4.	A	14.	A
5.	B	15.	C
6.	B	16.	C
7.	A	17.	B
8.	D	18.	C
9.	B	19.	D
10.	C	20.	C

21.	C
22.	B
23.	C
24.	B
25.	A

TEST 3

DIRECTIONS: Each question or incomplete statement is followed by several suggested answers or completions. Select the one that BEST answers the question or completes the statement. *PRINT THE LETTER OF THE CORRECT ANSWER IN THE SPACE AT THE RIGHT.*

Questions 1-6.

DIRECTIONS: Questions 1 through 6 are to be answered SOLELY on the basis of the following passage.

  A folder is made of a sheet of heavy paper (manila, kraft, pressboard, or red rope stock) that has been folded once so that the back is about one-half inch higher than the front. Folders are larger than the papers they contain in order to protect them. Two standard folder sizes are *letter size* for papers that are 8½" x 11" and *legal cap* for papers that are 8½" x 13".
  Folders are cut across the top in two ways: so that the back is straight (straight-cut) or so that the back has a tab that projects above the top of the folder. Such tabs bear captions that identify the contents of each folder. Tabs vary in width and position. The tabs of a set of folders that are *one-half cut* are half the width of the folder and have only two positions.
  One-third cut folders have three positions, each tab occupying a third of the width of the folder. Another standard tabbing is *one-fifth cut*, which has five positions. There are also folders with *two-fifths cut*, with the tabs in the third and fourth or fourth and fifth positions.

1. Of the following, the BEST title for the above passage is 1.____
  A. Filing Folders   B. Standard Folder Sizes
  C. The Uses of the Folder   D. The Use of Tabs

2. According to the above passage, one of the standard folder sizes is called 2.____
  A. Kraft cut   B. legal cap
  C. one-half cut   D. straight-cut

3. According to the above passage, tabs are GENERALLY placed along the _____ of the folder. 3.____
  A. back   B. front   C. left side   D. right side

4. According to the above passage, a tab is GENERALLY used to 4.____
  A. distinguish between standard folder sizes
  B. identify the contents of a folder
  C. increase the size of the folder
  D. protect the papers within the folder

5. According to the above passage, a folder that is two-fifths cut has _____ tabs. 5.____
  A. no   B. two   C. three   D. five

6. According to the above passage, one reason for making folders larger than the papers they contain is that
   A. only a certain size folder can be made from heavy paper
   B. they will protect the papers
   C. they will aid in setting up a tab system
   D. the back of the folder must be higher than the front

6.____

Questions 7-15.

DIRECTIONS: Questions 7 through 15 are to be answered SOLELY on the basis of the following passage.

The City University of New York traces its origins to 1847, when the Free Academy, which later became City College, was founded as the first tuition-free municipal college. City and Hunter Colleges were placed under the direction of the Board of Higher Education in 1926, and Brooklyn and Queens Colleges were subsequently added to the system of municipal colleges. In 1955, Staten Island Community College, the first of the two-year colleges sponsored by the Board of Higher Education under the program of the State University of New York, joined the system.

In 1961, the four senior colleges and three community colleges then under the jurisdiction of the Board of Higher Education became the City University of New York, and a University Graduate Division was organized to offer programs leading to the Ph.D. Since then, the university has undergone even more rapid growth. Today, it consists of nine senior colleges, an upper division college which admits students at the junior level, eight community colleges, a graduate division, and an affiliated medical center.

In the summer of 1969, the Board of Higher Education resolved that the time had come to commit the resources of the university to meeting an urgent social need—unrestricted access to higher education for all youths of the City. Determined to prevent the waste of human potential represented by the thousands of high school graduates whose limited educational opportunities left them unable to meet existing admission standards, the Board moved to adopt a policy of Open Admissions. It was their judgment that the best way of determining whether a potential student can benefit from college work is to admit him to college, provide him with the learning assistance he needs, and then evaluate his performance.

Beginning with the class of June 1970, every New York City resident who received a high school diploma from a public or private high school was guaranteed a place in one of the colleges of City University.

7. Of the following, the BEST title for the above passage is
   A. A Brief History of the City University
   B. High Schools and the City University
   C. The Components of the University
   D. Tuition-free Colleges

7.____

8. According to the above passage, which one of the following colleges of the City University was ORIGINALLY called the Free Academy?
   A. Brooklyn College   B. City College
   C. Hunter College   D. Queens College

8.____

9. According to the above passage, the system of municipal colleges became the City University of New York in
   A. 1926   B. 1955   C. 1961   D. 1969

10. According to the above passage, Staten Island Community College came under the jurisdiction of the Board of Higher Education
    A. 6 years after a Graduate Division was organized
    B. 8 years before the adoption of the Open Admissions Policy
    C. 29 years after Brooklyn and Queens Colleges
    D. 29 years after City and Hunter Colleges

11. According to the above passage, the Staten Island Community College is
    A. a graduate division center
    B. a senior college
    C. a two-year college
    D. an upper division college

12. According to the above passage, the TOTAL number of colleges, divisions, and affiliated branches of the City University is
    A. 18   B. 19   C. 20   D. 21

13. According to the above passage, the Open Admissions Policy is designed to determine whether a potential student will benefit from college by PRIMARILY
    A. discouraging competition for placement in the City University among high school students
    B. evaluating his performance after entry into college
    C. lowering admission standards
    D. providing learning assistance before entry into college

14. According to the above passage, the FIRST class to be affected by the Open Admissions Policy was the
    A. high school class which graduated in January 1970
    B. City University class which graduated in June 1970
    C. high school class when graduated in June 1970
    D. City University class when graduated in June 1970

15. According to the above passage, one of the reasons that the Board of Higher Education initiated the policy of Open Admission was to
    A. enable high school graduates with a background of limited educational opportunities to enter college
    B. expand the growth of the City University so as to increase the number and variety of degrees offered
    C. provide a social resource to the qualified youth of the City
    D. revise admission standards to meet the needs of the City

Questions 16-18.

DIRECTIONS: Questions 16 through 18 are to be answered SOLELY on the basis of the following passage.

Hereafter, all probationary students interested in transferring to community college career programs (associate degrees) from liberal arts programs in senior colleges (bachelor degrees) will be eligible for such transfers if they have completed no more than three semesters.
For students with averages 1.5 or above, transfer will be automatic. Those with 1.0 to 1.5 averages can transfer provisionally and will be required to make substantial progress during the first semester in the career program. Once transfer has taken place, only those courses in which passing grades were received will be computed in the community college grade-point average.
No request for transfer will be accepted from probationary students wishing to enter the liberal arts programs at the community college.

16. According to the above passage, the one of the following which is the BEST statement concerning the transfer of probationary students is that a probationary student
    A. may transfer to a career program at the end of one semester
    B. must complete three semester hours before he is eligible for transfer
    C. is not eligible to transfer to a career program
    D. is eligible to transfer to a liberal arts program

16._____

17. Which of the following is the BEST statement of academic evaluation for transfer purposes in the case of probationary students?
    A. No probationary student with an average under 1.5 may transfer.
    B. A probationary student with an average of 1.3 may not transfer.
    C. A probationary student with an average of 1.6 may transfer.
    D. A probationary student with an average of .8 may transfer on a provisional basis.

17._____

18. It is MOST likely that, of the following, the next degree sought by one who already holds the Associate in Science degree would be a(n) _____ degree.
    A. Assistantship in Science   B. Associate in Applied Science
    C. Bachelor of Science   D. Doctor of Philosophy

18._____

Questions 19-20.

DIRECTIONS: Questions 19 and 20 are to be answered SOLELY on the basis of the following passage.

Auto: Auto travel requires prior approval by the President and/or appropriate Dean and must be indicated in the *Request for Travel Authorization* form. Employees authorized to use personal autos on official College business will be reimbursed at the rate of 28¢ per mile for the first 500 miles driven and 18¢ per mile for mileage driven in excess of 500 mile. The Comptroller's Office may limit the amount of reimbursement to the expenditure that would have been made if a less expensive mode of transportation (railroad, airplane, bus, etc.) had been utilized. If this occurs, the traveler will have to pick up the excess expenditure as a personal expense.

Tolls, Parking Fees, and Parking Meter Fees are not reimbursable and many not be claimed.

19. Suppose that Professor T gives the office assistant the following memorandum: Used car for official trip to Albany, New York, and return. Distance from New York to Albany is 148 miles. Tolls were $3.50 each way. Parking garage cost $3.00. When preparing the Travel Expense Voucher for Professor T, the figure which should be claimed for transportation is
    A. $120.88   B. $113.88   C. $82.88   D. $51.44

19.____

20. Suppose that Professor V gives the office assistant the following memorandum: Used car for official trip to Pittsburgh, Pennsylvania, and return. Distance from New York to Pittsburgh is 350 miles. Tolls were $3.30, $11.40 going, and $3.30, $2.00 returning.
    When preparing the Travel Expense Voucher for Professor V, the figure which should be claimed for transportation is
    A. $225.40   B. $176.00   C. $127.40   D. $98.00

20.____

Questions 21-25.

DIRECTIONS: Questions 21 through 25 are to be answered SOLELY on the basis of the following passage.

For a period of nearly fifteen years, beginning in the mid-1950's, higher education sustained a phenomenal rate of growth. The factor principally responsible were continuing improvement in the rate of college entrance by high school graduates, a 50 percent increase in the size of the college-age (eighteen to twenty-one) group and—until about 1967—a rapid expansion of university research activity supported by the Federal government.

Today, as one looks ahead to the year 2010, it is apparent that each of these favorable stimuli will either be abated or turn into a negative factor. The rate of growth of the college-age group has already diminished; and from 2000 to 2005, the size of the college-age group has shrunk annually almost as fast as it grew from 1965 to 1970. From 2005 to 2010, this annual decrease will slow down so that by 2010 the age group will be about the same size as it was in 2009. This substantial net decrease in the size of the college-age group (from 1995 to 2010) will dramatically affect college enrollments since, currently, 83 percent of undergraduates are twenty-one and under, and another 11 percent are twenty-to to twenty-four.

21. Which one of the following factors is NOT mentioned in the above passage as contributing to the high rate of growth of higher education?
    A. A large increase in the size of the eighteen to twenty-one age group
    B. The equalization of educational opportunities among socio-economic groups
    C. The Federal budget impact on research and development spending in the higher education sector
    D. The increasing rate at which high school graduates enter college

21.____

22. Based on the information in the above passage, the size of the college-age group in 2010 will be
    A. larger than it was in 2009
    B. larger than it was in 1995
    C. smaller than it was in 2005
    D. about the same as it was in 2000

23. According to the above passage, the tremendous rate of growth of higher education started around
    A. 1950   B. 1955   C. 1960   D. 1965

24. The percentage of undergraduates who are over age 24 is MOST NEARLY
    A. 6%   B. 8%   C. 11%   D. 17%

25. Which one of the following conclusions can be substantiated by the information given in the above passage?
    A. The college-age group was about the same size in 2000 as it was in 1965.
    B. The annual decrease in the size of the college-age group from 2000 to 2005 is about the same as the annual increase from 1965 to 1970.
    C. The overall decrease in the size of the college-age group from 2000 to 2005 will be followed by an overall increase in its size from 2005 to 2010.
    D. The size of the college-age group is decreasing at a fairly constant rate from 1995 to 2010.

KEY (CORRECT ANSWERS)

1.	A		11.	C
2.	B		12.	C
3.	A		13.	B
4.	B		14.	C
5.	B		15.	A
6.	B		16.	A
7.	A		17.	C
8.	B		18.	C
9.	C		19.	C
10.	D		20.	B

21. B
22. C
23. B
24. A
25. B

PREPARING WRITTEN MATERIAL

PARAGRAPH REARRANGEMENT
COMMENTARY

The sentences that follow are in scrambled order. You are to rearrange them in proper order and indicate the letter choice containing the correct answer at the space at the right.

Each group of sentences in this section is actually a paragraph presented in scrambled order. Each sentence in the group has a place in that paragraph; no sentence is to be left out. You are to read each group of sentences and decide upon the best order in which to put the sentences so as to form a well-organized paragraph.

The questions in this section measure the ability to solve a problem when all the facts relevant to its solution are not given.

More specifically, certain positions of responsibility and authority require the employee to discover connection between events sometimes, apparently, unrelated. In order to do this, the employee will find it necessary to correctly infer that unspecified events have probably occurred or are likely to occur. This ability becomes especially important when action must be taken on incomplete information.

Accordingly, these questions require competitors to choose among several suggested alternatives, each of which presents a different sequential arrangement of the events. Competitors must choose the MOST logical of the suggested sequences.

In order to do so, they may be required to draw on general knowledge to infer missing concepts or events that are essential to sequencing the given events. Competitors should be careful to infer only what is essential to the sequence. The plausibility of the wrong alternatives will always require the inclusion of unlikely events or of additional chains of events which are NOT essential to sequencing the given events.

It's very important to remember that you are looking for the best of the four possible choices, and that the best choice of all may not even be one of the answers you're given to choose from.

There is no one right way to solve these problems. Many people have found it helpful to first write out the order of the sentences, as they would have arranged them, on their scrap paper before looking at the possible answers. If their optimum answer is there, this can save them some time. If it isn't, this method can still give insight into solving the problem. Others find it most helpful to just go through each of the possible choices, contrasting each as they go along. You should use whatever method feels comfortable and works for you.

While most of these types of questions are not that difficult, we've added a higher percentage of the difficult type, just to give you more practice. Usually there are only one or two questions on this section that contain such subtle distinctions that you're unable to answer confidently. And you then may find yourself stuck deciding between two possible choices, neither of which you're sure about.

PREPARING WRITTEN MATERIAL
EXAMINATION SECTION
TEST 1

DIRECTIONS: The following groups of sentences need to be arranged in an order that makes sense. Select the letter preceding the sequence that represents the BEST sentence order. *PRINT THE LETTER OF THE CORRECT ANSWER IN THE SPACE AT THE RIGHT.*

1. I. A large Naval station on Alameda Island, near Oakland, held many warships in port, and the War Department was worried that if the bridge were to be blown up by the enemy, passage to and from the bay would be hopelessly blocked.
    II. Though many skeptics were opposed to the idea of building such an enormous bridge, the most vocal opposition came from a surprising source: the United States War Department.
    III. The War Department's concerns led to a showdown at San Francisco City Hall between Strauss and the Secretary of War, who demanded to know what would happen if a military enemy blew up the bridge.
    IV. In 1933, by submitting a construction cost estimate of $17 million, an engineer named Joseph Strauss won the contract to build the Golden Gate Bridge of San Francisco, which would then become one of the world's largest bridges.
    V. Strauss quickly ended the debate by explaining that the Golden Gate Bridge was to be a suspension bridge, whose roadway would hang in the air from cables strung between two huge towers, and would immediately sink into three hundred feet of water if it were destroyed.
    The BEST order is:
    A. II, III, I, IV, V   B. I, II, III, V, IV   C. IV, II, I, III, V   D. IV, I, III, V, II

    1.____

2. I. Plastic surgeons have already begun to use virtual reality to map out the complex nerve and tissue structures of a particular patient's face, in order to prepare for delicate surgery.
    II. A virtual reality program responds to these movements by adjusting the images that a person sees on a screen or through goggles, thereby creating an "interactive" world in which a person can see and touch three-dimensional graphic objects.
    III. No more than a computer program that is designed to build and display graphic images, the virtual reality program takes graphic programs a step further by sensing a person's head and body movements.
    IV. The computer technology known as virtual reality, now in its very first stages of development, is already revolutionizing some aspects of contemporary life.
    V. Virtual reality computers are also being used by the space program, most recently to simulate conditions for the astronauts who were launched on a repair mission to the Hubble telescope.

    2.____

The BEST order is:
A. IV, II, I, V, III   B. III, I, V, II, IV   C. IV, III, II, I, V   D. III, I, II, IV, V

3. I. Before you plant anything, the soil in your plant bed should be carefully raked level, a small section at a time, and any clods or rocks that can't be broken up should be removed.
   II. Your plant should be placed in a hole that will position it at the same level it was at the nursery, and a small indentation should be pressed into the soil around the plant in order to hold water near its roots.
   III. Before placing the plant in the soil, lightly separate any roots that may have been matted together in the container, cutting away any thick masses that can't be separated, so that the remaining roots will be able to grow outward.
   IV. After the bed is ready, remove your plant from its container by turning it upside down and tapping or pushing on the bottom —never remove it by pulling on the plant.
   V. When you bring home a small plant in an individual container from the nursery, there are several things to remember while preparing to plant it in your own garden.
   The BEST order is:
   A. V, IV, III, II, I   B. V, II, IV, III, II   C. I, IV, II, III, V   D. I, IV, V, II, III

3.____

4. I. The motte and its tower were usually built first, so that sentries could use it as a lookout to warn the castle workers of any danger that might approach the castle.
   II. Though the moat and palisade offered the bailey a good deal of protection, it was linked to the motte by a set of stairs that led to a retractable drawbridge at the motte's gate, to enable people to evacuate onto the motte in case of an attack.
   III. The motte of these early castles was a fortified hill, sometimes as high as one hundred feet, on which stood a palisade and tower.
   IV. The bailey was a clear, level spot below the motte, also enclosed by a palisade, which in turn was surrounded by a large trench or moat.
   V. The earliest castles built in Europe were not the magnificent stone giants that still tower over much of the European landscape, but simpler wooden constructions called motte-and-bailey castles.
   The BEST order is:
   A. V, III, I, IV, II   B. V, IV, I, II, III   C. I, IV, III, II, V   D. I, III, II, IV, V

4.____

5. I. If an infant is left alone or abandoned for a short while, its immediate response is to cry loudly, accompanying its screams with aggressive flailing of its legs and limbs.
   II. If a child has been abandoned for a longer period of time, it becomes completely still and quiet, as if realizing that now its only chance for survival is to shut its mouth and remain motionless.
   III. Along with their intense fear of the dark, the crying behavior of human infants offers insights into how prehistoric newborn children might have evolved instincts that would prevent them from becoming victims of predators.

5.____

IV. This behavior often surprises people who enter a hospital's maternity ward for the first time and encounter total silence from a roomful of infants.

V. This violent screaming response is quite different from an infant's cries of discomfort or hunger, and seems to serve as either the child's first line of defense against an unwanted intruder, or a desperate attempt to communicate its position to the mother.

The BEST order is:
A. III, II, IV, I, V   B. III, I, V, II, IV   C. I, V, IV, II, III   D. II, IV, I, V, III

6. I. When two cats meet who are strangers, their first actions and gestures determine who the "dominant" cat will be, at least for the time being.

II. Unlike dogs, cats are typically a solitary animal species who avoid social interaction, but they do display specific social responses to each other upon meeting.

III. This is unlikely, however; before such a point of open hostility is reached, one of the cats will usually take the "submissive" position of crouching down while looking away from the other dat.

IV. If a cat desires dominance or sees the other cat as a threat to its territory, it will stare directly at the intruder with a lowered tail.

V. If the other cat responds with a similar gesture, or with the strong defensive posture of an arched back, laid-back ears and raised tail, a fight or chase is likely if neither cat gives in.

The BEST order is:
A. IV, II, I, V, III   B. I, II, IV, V, III   C. I, IV, V, III, II   D. II, I, IV, V, III

7. I. A star or planet's gravitational force can best be explained in this way: anything passing through this "dent" in space will veer toward the star or planet as if it were rolling into a hole.

II. Objects that are massive or heavy, such as stars or planets, "sink" into this surface, creating a sort of dent or concavity in the surrounding space.

III. Black holes, the most massive objects known to exist in space, create dents so large and deep that the space surrounding them actually folds in on itself, preventing anything that falls in —even light —from ever escaping again.

IV. The sort of dent a star or planet makes depends on how massive it is; planets generally have weak gravitational pulls, but stars, which are larger and heavier, make a bigger "dent" that will attract more matter.

V. In outer space, the force of gravity works as if the surrounding space is a soft, flat surface.

The BEST order is:
A. III, V, II, I, IV   B. III, IV, I, V, II   C. V, II, I, IV, III   D. I, V, II, IV, III

8. I. Eventually, the society of Kyoto gave the world one of its first and greatest novels when Japan's most promising writer, Lady Murasaki Shikibu, wrote her chronicle of Kyoto's society, *The Tale of Genji*, which preceded the first European novels by more than 500 years.

II. The society of Kyoto was dedicated to the pleasures of art; the courtiers experimented with new and colorful methods of sculpture, painting, writing, decorative gardening, and even making clothes.

III. Japanese culture began under the powerful authority of Chinese Buddhism, which influenced every aspect of Japanese life from religion to politics and art.
IV. This new, vibrant culture was so sophisticated that all the people in Kyoto's imperial court considered themselves poets, and the line between life and art hardly existed —lovers corresponded entirely through written verses, and even government officials communicated by writing poems to each other.
V. In the eighth century, when the emperor established the town of Kyoto as the capital of the Japanese empire, Japanese society began to develop its own distinctive style.
The BEST order is:
  A. V, II, IV, I, III   B. II, I, V, IV, III   C. V, III, IV, I, II   D. III, V, II, IV, I

9. I. Instead of wheels, the HSST uses two sets of magnets, one which sits on the track, and another that is carried by the train; these magnets generate an identical magnetic field which forces the two sets apart.
II. In the last few decades, railway travel has become less popular throughout the world, because it is much slower than travel by airplane, and not much less expensive.
III. The HSST's designers say that the train can take passengers from one town to another as quickly as a jet plane —while consuming less than half the energy.
IV. This repellent effect is strong enough to lift the entire train above the trackway, and the train, literally traveling on air, rockets along at speeds of up to 300 miles per hour.
V. The revolutionary technology of magnetic levitation, currently being tested by Japan's experimental HSST (High Speed Surface Transport), may yet bring passenger trains back from the dead.
The BEST order is:
  A. II, V, I, IV, III   B. II, I, IV, III, V   C. V, II, III, I, IV   D. V, I, III, IV, II

9.____

10. I. When European countries first began to colonize the African continent, their impression of the African people was of a vast group of loosely organized tribal societies, without any great centralized source of power or wealth.
II. The legend of Timbuktu persisted until the nineteenth century, when a French adventurer visited Timbuktu and found that raids by neighboring tribesmen had made the city a shadow of its former self.
III. In the fifteenth century, when the stories of travelers who had traveled Africa's Sudan region began circulating around Europe, this impression began to change.
IV. In 1470, an Italian merchant named Benedetto Dei traveled to Timbuktu and confirmed these rumors, describing a thriving metropolis where rich and poor people worshipped together in the city's many ornate mosques — there was even a university in Timbuktu, much like its European counterparts, where African scholars pursued their studies in the arts and sciences.

10.____

V. The travelers' legends told of an enormous city in the western Sudan, Timbuktu, where the streets were crowded with goods brought by faraway caravans, and where there was a stone palace as large as any in Europe.

The BEST order is:
A. III, V, I, IV, II B. I, II, IV, III, V C. I, III, V, IV, II D. II, I, III, IV, V

11. I. Also, our reference points in sighting the moon make us believe that its size is changing; when the moon is rising through the trees, it seems huge, because our brains unconsciously compare the size of the moon with the size of the trees in the foreground.
    II. To most people, the sky itself appears more distant at the horizon than directly overhead, and if the moon's size—which remains constant—is projected from the horizon, the apparent distance of the horizon makes the moon look bigger.
    III. Up higher in the sky, the moon is set against tiny stars in the background, which will make the moon seem smaller.
    IV. People often wonder why the moon becomes bigger when it approaches the horizon, but most scientists agree that this is a complicated optical illusion, produced by at least three factors.
    V. The moon illusion may also be partially explained by a phenomenon that has nothing to do with errors in our perception—light that enters the earth's atmosphere is sometimes refracted, and so the atmosphere may act as a kind of magnifying glass for the moon's image.

    The BEST order is:
    A. IV, III, V, II, I B. IV, II, I, III, V C. V, II, I, III, IV D. II, I, III, IV, V

11.____

12. I. When the Native Americans were introduced to the horses used by white explorers, they were amazed at their new alternative—here was an animal that was strong and swift, would patiently carry a person or other loads on its back, and they later discovered, was right at home on the plains.
    II. Before the arrival of European explorers to North America, the natives of the American plains used large dogs to carry their travois-long lodgepoles loaded with clothing, gear, and food.
    III. These horses, it is now known, were not really strangers to North America; the very first horses originated here, on this continent, tens of thousands of years ago, and migrated into Asia across the Bering Land Bridge, a strip of land that used to link our continent with the Eastern world.
    IV. At first, the natives knew so little about horses that at least one tribe tried to feed their new animals pieces of dried meat and animal fat, and were surprised when the horses turned their heads away and began to eat the grass of the prairie.
    V. The American horse eventually became extinct, but its Asian cousins were reintroduced to the New World when the European explorers brought them to live among the Native Americans.

    The BEST order is:
    A. II, I, IV, III, V B. II, IV, I, III, V C. I, II, IV, III, V D. I, III, V, II, IV

12.____

13. I. The dress worn by the dancer is believed to have been adorned in the past by shells which would strike each other as the dancer performed, creating a lovely sound.
   II. Today's jingle-dress is decorated with the tin lids of snuff cans, which are rolled into cones and sewn onto the dress,
   III. During the jingle-dress dance, the dancer must blend complicated footwork with a series of gentle hos that cause the cones to jingle in rhythm to a drumbeat.
   IV. When contemporary Native American tribes meet for a pow-wow, one of the most popular ceremonies to take place is the women's jingle-dress dance.
   V. Besides being more readily available than shells, the lids are thought by many dancers to create a softer, more subtle sound.
   The BEST order is:
   A. II, IV, V, I, III   B. IV, II, I, III, V   C. II, I, III, V, IV   D. IV, I, II, V, III

14. I. If a homeowner lives where seasonal climates are extreme, deciduous shade trees—which will drop their leaves in the winter and allow sunlight to pass through the windows—should be planted near the southern exposure in order to keep the house cool during the summer.
   II. This trajectory is shorter and lower in the sky than at any other time of year during the winter, when a house most requires heating; the northern-facing parts of a house do not receive any direct sunlight at all.
   III. In designing an energy-efficient house, especially in colder climates, it is important to remember that most of the house's windows should face south.
   IV. Though the sun always rises in the east and sets in the west, the sun of the northern hemisphere is permanently situated in the southern portion of the sky.
   V. The explanation for why so many architects and builders want this "southern exposure" is related to the path of the sun in the sky.
   The BEST order is:
   A. III, I, V, IV, II   B. III, V, IV, II, I   C. I, III, IV, II, V   D. I, II, V, IV, III

15. I. His journeying lasted twenty-four years and took him over an estimated 75,000 miles, a distance that would not be surpassed by anyone other than Magellan—who sailed around the world—for another six hundred years.
   II. Perhaps the most far-flung of these lesser-known travelers was Ibn Batuta, an African Moslem who left his birthplace of Tangier in the summer of 1325
   III. Ibn Batuta traveled all over Africa and Asia, from Niger to Peking, and to the islands of Maldive and Indonesia.
   IV. However, a few explorers of the Eastern world logged enough miles and adventures to make Marco Polo's voyage look like an evening stroll.
   V. In America, the most well-known of the Old World's explorers are usually Europeans such as Marco Polo, the Italian who brought many elements of Chinese culture to the Western world.
   The BEST order is:
   A. V, IV, II, III, I   B. V, IV, III, II, I   C. III, II, I, IV, V   D. II, III, I, IV, V

16. I. In the rainforests of South America, a rare species of frog practices a reproductive method that is entirely different from this standard process.
    II. She will eventually carry each of the tadpoles up into the canopy and drop each into its own little pool, where it will be easy to locate and safe from most predators.
    III. After fertilization, the female of the species, who lives almost entirely on the forest floor, lays between 2 and 16 eggs among the leaf litter at the base of a tree, and stands watch over these eggs until they hatch.
    IV. Most frogs are pond-dwellers who are able to deposit hundreds of eggs in the water and then leave them alone, knowing that enough eggs have been laid to insure the survival of some of their offspring.
    V. Once the tadpoles emerge, the female backs in among them, and a tadpole will wriggle onto her back to be carried high into the forest canopy, where the female will deposit it in a little pool of water cupped in the leaf of a plant.
    The BEST order is:
    A. I, IV, III, II, V   B. I, III, V, II, IV   C. IV, III, II, V, I   D. IV, I, III, V, II

17. I. Eratosthenes had heard from travelers that at exactly noon on June 21, in the ancient city of Aswan, Egypt, the sun cast no shadow in a well, which meant that the sun must be directly overhead.
    II. He knew the sun always cast a shadow in Alexandria, and so he figured that if he could measure the length of an Alexandria shadow at the time when there was no shadow in Aswan, he could calculate the angle of the sun, and therefore the circumference of the earth.
    III. The evidence for a round earth was not new in 1492; in fact, Eratosthenes, an Alexandrian geographer who lived nearly sixteen centuries before Columbus's voyage (275-195 B.C.), actually developed a method for calculating the circumference of the earth that is still in use today.
    IV. Eratosthenes's method was correct, but his result—28,700 miles—was about 15 percent too high, probably because of the inaccurate ancient methods of keeping time, and because Aswan was not due south of Alexandria, as Eratosthenes had believed.
    V. When Christopher Columbus sailed across the Atlantic Ocean for the first time in 1492, there were still some people in the world who ignored scientific evidence and believed that the earth was flat, rather than round.
    The BEST order is:
    A. I, II, V, III, IV   B. V, III, IV, I, II   C. V, III, I, II, IV   D. III, V, I, II, IV

18. I. The first name for the child is considered a trial naming, often impersonal and neutral, such as the Ngoni name *Chabwera*, meaning "it has arrived."
    II. This sort of name is not due to any parental indifference to the child, but is a kind of silent recognition of Africa's sometimes high infant death rate; most parents ease the pain of losing a child with the belief that it is not really a person until it has been given a final name.
    III In many tribal African societies, families often give two different names to their children, at different periods in time.
    IV. After the trial naming period has subsided and it is clear that the child will survive, the parents choose a final name for the child, an act that symbolically completes the act of birth.

V. In fact, some African first-given names are explicitly uncomplimentary, translating as "I am dead" or "I am ugly," in order to avoid the jealousy of ancestral spirits who might wish to take a child that is especially healthy or attractive.

The BEST order is:
A. III, I, II, V, IV B. III, IV, II, I, V C. IV, III, I, II, V D. IV, V, III, I, II

19.
I. Though uncertain of the definite reasons for this behavior, scientists believe the birds digest the clay in order to counteract toxins contained in the seeds of certain fruits that are eaten by macaws.
II. For example, all macaws flock to riverbanks at certain times of the year to eat the clay that is found in river mud.
III. The macaws of South America are not only among the largest and most beautifully colored of the world's flying birds, but they are also one of the smartest.
IV. It is believed that macaws are forced to resort to these toxic fruits during the dry season, when foods are more scarce.
V. The macaw's intelligence has led to intense study by scientists, who have discovered some macaw behaviors that have not yet been explained.

The BEST order is:
A. III, IV, I, II, V B. III, V, II, I, IV C. V, II, I, IV, III D. IV, I, II, III, V

19.____

20.
I. Although Maggie Kuhn has since passed away, the Gray Panthers are still waging a campaign to reinstate the historical view of the elderly as people whose experience allows them to make their greatest contribution in their later years.
II. In 1972, an elderly woman named Maggie Kuhn responded to this sort of treatment by forming a group called the Gray Panthers, an organization of both old and young adults with the common goal of creating change.
III. This attitude is reflected strongly in the way elderly people are treated by our society; many are forced into early retirement, or are placed in rest homes in which they are isolated from their communities.
IV. Unlike most other cultures around the world, Americans tend to look upon old age with a sense of dread and sadness.
V. Kuhn believed that when the elderly are forced to withdraw into lives that lack purpose, society loses one of its greatest resources: people who have a lifetime of experience and wisdom to offer their communities.

The BEST order is:
A. IV, III, II, V, I B. IV, II, I, III, V C. II, IV, III, V, I D. II, I, IV, III, V

20.____

21.
I. The current theory among most anthropologists is that humans evolved from apes who lived in trees near the grasslands of Africa.
II. Still, some anthropologists insist that such an invention was necessary for the survival of early humans, and point to the Kung Bushmen of central Africa as a society in which the sling is still used in this way.
III. Two of these inventions—fire, and weapons such as spears and clubs—were obvious defenses against predators, and there is archaeological evidence to support the theory of their use.

21.____

IV. Once people had evolved enough to leave the safety of trees and walk upright, they needed the protection of several inventions in order to survive.
V. But another invention, a feather or fiber sling that allowed mothers to carry children while leaving their hands free to gather roots or berries, would certainly have decomposed and left behind no trace of itself.

The BEST order is:
A. I, II, III, V, IV B. IV, I, II, III, V C. I, IV, III, V, II D. IV, III, V, II, I

22. I. The person holding the bird should keep it in hot water up to its neck, and the person cleaning should work a mild solution of dishwashing liquid into the bird's plumage, paying close attention to the head and neck.
II. When rinsing the bird, after all the oil has been removed, the running water should be directed against the lay of its feathers, until water begins to bead off the surface of the feathers—a sign that all the detergent has been rinsed out.
III. If you have rescued a sea bird from an oil spill and want to restore it to clean and normal living, you need a large sink, a constant supply of running hot water (a little over 100°F), and regular dishwashing liquid.
IV. This cleaning with detergent solution should be repeated as many times as it takes to remove all traces of oil from the bird's feathers, sometime over a period of several days.
V. But before you begin to clean the bird, you must find a partner because cleaning an oiled bird is a two-person job.

The BEST order is:
A. III, I, II, IV, V B. III, V, I, IV, II C. III, I, IV, V, II D. III, IV, V, I, II

23. I. The most difficult time of year for the Tsaatang is the spring calving, when the reindeer leave their wintering ground and rush to their accustomed calving place, without stopping by night or by day.
II. Reindeer travel in herds, and though some animals are tamed by the Tsaatang for riding or milking, the herds are allowed to roam free.
III. This journey is hard for the Tsaatang, who carry all their possessions with them, but once it's over it proves worthwhile; the Tsaatang can immediately begin to gather milk from reindeer cows who have given birth.
IV. The Tsaatang, a small tribe who live in the far northwest corner of Mongolia, practice a lifestyle that is completely dependent on the reindeer, their main resource for food, clothing, and transport.
V. The people must follow their yearly migrations, living in portable shelters that resemble Native American tepees.

The BEST order is:
A. I, III, II, V, IV B. I, IV, II, V, III C. IV, I, III, V, II D. IV II, V, I, III

24. I. The Romans later improved this system by installing these heated pipe networks throughout walls and ceilings, supplying heat to even the uppermost floors of a building—a system that, to this day, hasn't been much improved.
II. Air-conditioning, the method by which humans control indoor temperatures, was practiced much earlier than most people think.

III. The earliest heating devices other than open fires were used in 350 B.C. by the ancient Greeks, who directed air that had been heated by underground fires into baked clay pipes that ran under the floor.
IV. Ironically, the first successful cooling system, patented in England in 1831, used fire as its main energy source—fires were lit in the attic of a building, creating an updraft of air that drew cool air into the building through ducts that had underground openings near the river Thames.
V. Cooling buildings was more of a challenge, and wasn't attempted until 1500: a water-based system, designed by Leonardo da Vinci, does not appear to have been successful, since it was never used again.

The BEST order is:
A. III, V, IV, I, II   B. III, I, II, V, IV   C. II, III, I, V, IV   D. IV, II, III, I, V

25. I. Cold, dry air from Canada passes over the Rocky Mountains and sweeps down onto the plains, where it collides with warm, moist air from the waters of the Gulf of Mexico, and when the two air masses meet, the resulting disturbance sometimes forms a violent funnel cloud that strikes the earth and destroys virtually everything in its path.
II. Hurricanes, storms which are generally not this violent and last much longer, are usually given names by meteorologists, but this tradition cannot be applied to tornados, which have a life span measured in minutes and disappear in the same way as they are born—unnamed.
III. A tornado funnel forms rotating columns of air whose speed reaches three hundred miles an hour—a speed that can only be estimated, because no wind-measuring devices in the direct path of a storm have ever survived.
IV. The natural phenomena known as tornados occur primarily over the Midwestern grasslands of the United States.
V. It is here, meteorologists tell us, that conditions for the formation of tornados are sometimes perfect during the spring months.

The BEST order is:
A. II, IV, V, I, III   B. II, III, I, V, IV   C. IV, V, I, III, II   D. IV, III, I, V, II

KEY (CORRECT ANSWERS)

1. C
2. C
3. B
4. A
5. B

6. D
7. C
8. D
9. A
10. C

11. B
12. A
13. D
14. B
15. A

16. D
17. C
18. A
19. B
20. A

21. C
22. B
23. D
24. C
25. C

EXAMINATION SECTION
TEST 1

DIRECTIONS: The sentences that follow are in scrambled order. You are to rearrange them in proper order and indicate the letter choice containing the correct answer. *PRINT THE LETTER OF THE CORRECT ANSWER IN THE SPACE AT THE RIGHT.*

1. Below are four statements labeled W, X, Y and Z. 1.____
   W. He was a strict and fanatic drillmaster.
   X. The word is always used in a derogatory sense and generally shows resentment and anger on the part of the user.
   Y. It is from the name of this Frenchman that we derive our English word, martinet.
   Z. Jean Martinet was the Inspector-General of Infantry during the reign of King Louis XIV.
   The PROPER order in which these sentences should be placed in a paragraph is:
      A. X, Z, W, Y   B. X, Z, Y, W   C. Z, W, Y, X   D. Z, Y, W, X

2. In the following paragraph, the sentences, which are numbered, have been jumbled. 2.____
   I. Since then it has undergone changes.
   II. It was incorporated in 1955 under the laws of the State of New York.
   III. Its primary purposes, a cleaner city, has, however, remained the same.
   IV. The Citizens Committee works in cooperation with the Mayor's Inter-departmental Committee for a Clean City. 3.____
   The order in which these sentences should be arranged to form a well-organized paragraph is:
      A. II, IV, I, III   B. III, IV, I, II   C. IV, II, I, III   D. IV, III, II, I

Questions 3-5.

DIRECTIONS: The sentences listed below are part of a meaningful paragraph but they are not given in their proper order. You are to decide what would be the BEST order in which to put the sentences so as to form a well-organized paragraph. Each sentence has a place in the paragraph; there are no extra sentences. You are then to answer Questions 3 through 5 inclusive on the basis of your rearrangements of these scrambled sentences into a properly organized paragraph.

In 1887 some insurance companies organized an Inspection Department to advise their clients on all phases of fire prevention and protection. Probably this has been due to the smaller annual fire losses in Great Britain than in the United States. It tests various fire prevention devices and appliances and determines manufacturing hazards and their safeguards. Fire research began earlier in the United States and is more advanced than in Great Britain. Later they established a laboratory specializing in electrical, mechanical, hydraulic, and chemical fields.

3. When the five sentences are arranged in proper order, the paragraph starts with the sentence which begins
   A. "In 1887..."   B. "Probably this..."   C. "It tests..."
   D. "Fire research..."   E. "Later they..."

4. In the last sentence listed above, "they" refers to
   A. the insurance companies
   B. the United States and Great Britain
   C. the Inspection Department
   D. clients
   E. technicians

5. When the above paragraph is properly arranged, it ends with the words
   A. "...and protection."
   B. "...the United States."
   C. "...their safeguards."
   D. "...in Great Britain."
   E. "...chemical fields."

KEY (CORRECT ANSWERS)

1. C
2. C
3. D
4. A
5. C

TEST 2

DIRECTIONS: In each of the questions numbered I through V, several sentences are given. For each question, choose as your answer the group of number that represents the MOST logical order of these sentences if they were arranged in paragraph form. *PRINT THE LETTER OF THE CORRECT ANSWER IN THE SPACE AT THE RIGHT.*

1. I. It is established when one shows that the landlord has prevented the tenant's enjoyment of his interest in the property leased.
    II. Constructive eviction is the result of a breach of the covenant of quiet enjoyment implied in all leases.
    III. In some parts of the United States, it is not complete until the tenant vacates within a reasonable time.
    IV. Generally, the acts must be of such serious and permanent character as to deny the tenant the enjoyment of his possessing rights.
    V. In this event, upon abandonment of the premises, the tenant's liability for that ceases.
    The CORRECT answer is:
    A. II, I, IV, III, V
    B. V, II, III, I, IV
    C. IV, III, I, II, V
    D. I, III, V, IV, II

    1.____

2. I. The powerlessness before private and public authorities that is the typical experience of the slum tenant is reminiscent of the situation of blue-collar workers all through the nineteenth century.
    II. Similarly, in recent years, this chapter of history has been reopened by anti-poverty groups which have attempted to organize slum tenants to enable them to bargain collectively with their landlords about the conditions of their tenancies.
    III. It is familiar history that many of the worker remedied their condition by joining together and presenting their demands collectively.
    IV. Like the workers, tenants are forced by the conditions of modern life into substantial dependence on these who possess great political aid and economic power.
    V. What's more, the very fact of dependence coupled with an absence of education and self-confidence makes them hesitant and unable to stand up for what they need from those in power.
    The CORRECT answer is:
    A. V, IV, I, II, III
    B. II, III, I, V, IV
    C. III, I, V, IV, II
    D. I, IV, V, III, II

    2.____

3. I. A railroad, for example, when not acting as a common carrier may contract away responsibility for its own negligence.
    II. As to a landlord, however, no decision has been found relating to the legal effect of a clause shifting the statutory duty of repair to the tenant.
    III. The courts have not passed on the validity of clauses relieving the landlord of this duty and liability.
    IV. They have, however, upheld the validity of exculpatory clauses in other types of contracts.

    3.____

131

V. Housing regulations impose a duty upon the landlord to maintain leased premises in safe condition.
VI. As another example, a bailee may limit his liability except for gross negligence, willful acts, or fraud.

The CORRECT answer is:
A. II, I, VI, IV, III, V
B. I, III, IV, V, VI, II
C. III, V, I, IV, II, VI
D. V, III, IV, I, VI, II

4.
I. Since there are only samples in the building, retail or consumer sales are generally eschewed by mart occupants, and in some instances, rigid controls are maintained to limit entrance to the mart only to those persons engaged in retailing.
II. Since World War I, in many larger cities, there has developed a new type of property, called the mart building.
III. It can, therefore, be used by wholesalers and jobbers for the display of sample merchandise.
IV. This type of building is most frequently a multi-storied, finished interior property which is a cross between a retail arcade and a loft building.
V. This limitation enables the mart occupants to ship the orders from another location after the retailer or dealer makes his selection from the samples.

The CORRECT answer is:
A. II, IV, III, I, V
B. IV, III, V, I, II
C. I, III, II, IV, V
D. I, IV, II, III, V

5.
I. In general, staff-line friction reduces the distinctive contribution of staff personnel.
II. The conflicts, however, introduce an uncontrolled element into the managerial system.
III. On the other hand, the natural resistance of the line to staff innovations probably usefully restrains over-eager efforts to apply untested procedures on a large scale.
IV. Under such conditions, it is difficult to know when valuable ideas are being sacrificed.
V. The relatively weak position of staff, requiring accommodation to the line, tends to restrict their ability to engage in free, experimental innovation.

The CORRECT answer is:
A. IV, II, III, I, V
B. I, V, III, II, IV
C. V, III, I, II, IV
D. II, I, IV, V, III

KEY (CORRECT ANSWERS)

1. A
2. D
3. D
4. A
5. B

TEST 3

DIRECTIONS: Questions 1 through 4 consist of six sentences which can be arranged in a logical sequence. For each question, select the choice which places the numbered sentences in the MOST logical sequent. *PRINT THE LETTER OF THE CORRECT ANSWER IN THE SPACE AT THE RIGHT.*

1.
   I. The burden of proof as to each issue is determined before trial and remains upon the same party throughout the trial.
   II. The jury is at liberty to believe one witness' testimony as against a number of contradictory witnesses.
   III. In a civil case, the party bearing the burden of proof is required to prove his contention by a fair preponderance of the evidence.
   IV. However, it must be noted that a fair preponderance of evidence does not necessarily mean a greater number of witnesses.
   V. The burden of proof is the burden which rests upon one of the parties to an action to persuade the trier of the facts, generally the jury, that a proposition he asserts is true.
   VI. If the evidence is equally balanced, or if it leaves the jury in such doubt as to be unable to decide the controversy either way, judgment must be given against the party upon whom the burden of proof rests.
   The CORRECT answer is:
   A. III, II, V, IV, I, VI   B. I, II, VI, V, III, IV
   C. III, IV, V, I, II, VI   D. V, I, III, VI, IV, II

   1.____

2.
   I. If a parent is without assets and is unemployed, he cannot be convicted of the crime of non-support of a child.
   II. The term "sufficient ability" has been held to mean sufficient financial ability.
   III. It does not matter if his unemployment is by choice or unavoidable circumstances.
   IV. If he fails to take any steps at all, he may be liable to prosecution for endangering the welfare of a child.
   V. Under the penal law, a parent is responsible for the support of his minor child only if the parent is "of sufficient ability."
   VI. An indigent parent may meet his obligation by borrowing money or by seeking aid under the provisions of the Social Welfare Law.
   The CORRECT answer is:
   A. VI, I, V, III, II, IV   B. I, III, V, II, IV, VI
   C. V, II, I, III, VI, IV   D. I, VI, IV, V, II, III

   2.____

3.
   I. Consider, for example, the case of a rabble rouser who urges a group of twenty people to go out and break the windows of a nearby factory.
   II. Therefore, the law fills the indicated gap with the crime of inciting to riot.
   III. A person is considered guilty of inciting to riot when he urges ten or more persons to engage in tumultuous and violent conduct of a kind likely to create public alarm.
   IV. However, if he has not obtained the cooperation of at least four people, he cannot be charged with unlawful assembly.

   3.____

133

V. The charge of inciting to riot was added to the law to cover types of conduct which cannot be classified as either the crime of "riot" or the crime of "unlawful assembly."
VI. If he acquires the acquiescence of at least four of them, he is guilty of unlawful assembly even if the project does not materialize.

The CORRECT answer is:
A. III, V, I, VI, IV, II
B. V, I, IV, VI, II, III
C. III, IV, I, V, II, VI
D. V, I, IV, VI, III, II

4. I. If, however, the rebuttal evidence presents an issue of credibility, it is for the jury to determine whether the presumption has, in fact, been destroyed.
II. Once sufficient evidence to the contrary is introduced, the presumption disappears from the trial.
III. The effect of a presumption is to place the burden upon the adversary to come forward with evidence to rebut the presumption.
IV. When a presumption is overcome and ceases to exist in the case, the fact or facts which gave rise to the presumption still remain.
V. Whether a presumption has been overcome is ordinarily a question for the court.
VI. Such information may furnish a basis for a logical inference.

The CORRECT answer is:
A. IV, VI, II, V, I, III
B. III, II, V, I, IV, VI
C. V, III, VI, IV, II, I
D. V, IV, I, II, VI, III

4.____

KEY (CORRECT ANSWERS)

1. D
2. C
3. A
4. B

PREPARING WRITTEN MATERIAL
EXAMINATION SECTION
TEST 1

DIRECTIONS: Each of the sentences in this test may be classified under one of the following four categories:
  A. *Incorrect* because of faulty grammar or sentence structure
  B. *Incorrect* because of faulty punctuation
  C. *Incorrect* because of faulty capitalization
  D. *Correct*

Examine each sentence carefully to determine under which of the above four options it is best classified. Then, in the space at the right, print the capital letter preceding the option which is the BEST of the four suggested above.

(Each incorrect sentence contains but one type of error. Consider a sentence to be correct if it contains none of the types of errors mentioned, even though there may be other correct ways of expressing the same thought.)

1. This fact, together with those brought out at the previous meeting, prove that the schedule is satisfactory to the employees. 1.____

2. Like many employees in scientific fields, the work of bookkeepers and accountants requires accuracy and neatness. 2.____

3. "What can I do for you," the secretary asked as she motioned to the visitor to take a seat. 3.____

4. Our representative, Mr. Charles will call on you next week to determine whether or not your claim has merit. 4.____

5. We expect you to return in the spring; please do not disappoint us. 5.____

6. Any supervisor, who disregards the just complaints of his subordinates, is remiss in the performance of his duty. 6.____

7. Because she took less than an hour for lunch is no reason for permitting her to leave before five o'clock. 7.____

8. "Miss Smith," said the supervisor, "Please arrange a meeting of the staff for two o'clock on Monday." 8.____

9. A private company's vacation and sick leave allowance usually differs considerably from a public agency. 9.____

10. Therefore, in order to increase the efficiency of operations in the department, a report on the recommended changes in procedures was presented to the departmental committee in charge of the program. 10.____

11. We told him to assign the work to whoever was available.   11.____

12. Since John was the most efficient of any other employee in the bureau, he   12.____
    received the highest service rating.

13. Only those members of the national organization who resided in the middle   13.____
    West attended the conference in Chicago.

14. The question of whether the office manager has as yet attained, or indeed   14.____
    can ever hope to secure professional status is one which has been discussed
    for years.

15. No one knew who to blame for the error which, we later discovered, resulted   15.____
    in a considerable loss of time.

KEY (CORRECT ANSWERS)

1.	A	6.	B	11.	D
2.	A	7.	A	12.	A
3.	B	8.	C	13.	C
4.	B	9.	A	14.	B
5.	D	10.	D	15.	A

TEST 2

DIRECTIONS: Each of the sentences in this test may be classified under one of the following four categories:
- A. *Incorrect* because of faulty grammar or sentence structure
- B. *Incorrect* because of faulty punctuation
- C. *Incorrect* because of faulty capitalization
- D. *Correct*

1. The National alliance of Businessmen is trying to persuade private businesses to hire youth in the summertime.   1._____

2. The supervisor who is on vacation, is in charge of processing vouchers.   2._____

3. The activity of the committee at its conferences is always stimulating.   3._____

4. After checking the addresses again, the letters went to the mailroom.   4._____

5. The director, as well as the employees, are interested in sharing the dividends.   5._____

KEY (CORRECT ANSWERS)

1. C
2. B
3. D
4. A
5. A

TEST 3

DIRECTIONS: In each of the following groups of sentences, one of the four sentences is faulty in grammar, punctuation, or capitalization. Select the INCORRECT sentence in each case.

1. A. Sailing down the bay was a thrilling experience for me.
   B. He was not consulted about your joining the club.
   C. This story is different than the one I told you yesterday.
   D. There is no doubt about his being the best player.

   1.____

2. A. He maintains there is but one road to world peace.
   B. It is common knowledge that a child sees much he is not supposed to see.
   C. Much of the bitterness might have been avoided if arbitration had been resorted to earlier in the meeting.
   D. The man decided it would be advisable to marry a girl somewhat younger than him.

   2.____

3. A. In this book, the incident I liked least is where the hero tries to put out the forest fire.
   B. Learning a foreign language will undoubtedly give a person a better understanding of his mother tongue.
   C. His actions made us wonder what he planned to do next.
   D. Because of the war, we were unable to travel during the summer vacation.

   3.____

4. A. The class had no sooner become interested in the lesson than the dismissal bell rang.
   B. There is little agreement about the kind of world to be planned at the peace conference.
   C. "Today," said the teacher, "we shall read 'The Wind in the Willows,' I am sure you'll like it.
   D. The terms of the legal settlement of the family quarrel handicapped both sides for many years.

   4.____

5. A. I was so surprised that I was not able to say a word.
   B. She is taller than any other member of the class.
   C. It would be much more preferable if you were never seen in his company.
   D. We had no choice but to excuse her for being late.

   5.____

KEY (CORRECT ANSWERS)

1. C
2. D
3. A
4. C
5. C

TEST 4

DIRECTIONS: In each of the following groups of sentences, one of the four sentences is faulty in grammar, punctuation, or capitalization. Select the INCORRECT sentence in each case.

1. A. Please send me these data at the earliest opportunity.
   B. The loss of their material proved to be a severe handicap.
   C. My principal objection to this plan is that it is impracticable.
   D. The doll had laid in the rain for an hour and was ruined.

1._____

2. A. The garden scissors, left out all night in the rain, were in a badly rusted condition.
   B. The girls felt bad about the misunderstanding which had arisen
   C. Sitting near the campfire, the old man told John and I about many exciting adventures he had had.
   D. Neither of us is in a position to undertake a task of that magnitude.

2._____

3. A. The general concluded that one of the three roads would lead to the besieged city.
   B. The children didn't, as a rule, do hardly anything beyond what they were told to do.
   C. The reason the girl gave for her negligence was that she had acted on the spur of the moment.
   D. The daffodils and tulips look beautiful in that blue vase.

3._____

4. A. If I was ten years older, I should be interested in this work.
   B. Give the prize to whoever has drawn the best picture.
   C. When you have finished reading the book, take it back to the library.
   D. My drawing is as good as or better than yours.

4._____

5. A. He asked me whether the substance was animal or vegetable.
   B. An apple which is unripe should not be eaten by a child.
   C. That was an insult to me who am your friend.
   D. Some spy must of reported the matter to the enemy.

5._____

6. A. Limited time makes quoting the entire message impossible.
   B. Who did she say was going?
   C. The girls in your class have dressed more dolls this year than we.
   D. There was such a large amount of books on the floor that I couldn't find a place for my rocking chair.

6._____

7. A. What with his sleeplessness and his ill health, he was unable to assume any responsibility for the success of the meeting.
   B. If I had been born in February, I should be celebrating my birthday soon.
   C. In order to prevent breakage, she placed a sheet of paper between each of the plates when she packed them.
   D. After the spring shower, the violets smelled very sweet.

7._____

2 (#4)

8. A. He had laid the book down very reluctantly before the end of the lesson. 8.____
   B. The dog, I am sorry to say, had lain on the bed all night.
   C. The cloth was first lain on a flat surface; then it was pressed with a hot iron.
   D. While we were in Florida, we lay in the sun until we were noticeably tanned.

9. A. If John was in New York during the recent holiday season, I have no doubt 9.____
      he spent most of the time with his parents.
   B. How could he enjoy the television program; the dog was barking and the
      baby was crying.
   C. When the problem was explained to the class, he must have been asleep.
   D. She wished that her new dress were finished so that she could go to the
      party.

10. A. The engine not only furnishes power but light and heat as well. 10.____
    B. You're aware that we've forgotten whose guilt was established, aren't you?
    C. Everybody knows that the woman made many sacrifices for her children.
    D. A man with his dog and gun is a familiar sight in this neighborhood.

KEY (CORRECT ANSWERS)

1. D   6. D
2. C   7. B
3. B   8. C
4. A   9. B
5. D   10. A

TEST 5

DIRECTIONS: Each of Questions 1 through 5 consists of a sentence which may be classified appropriately under one of the following four categories:
  A. *Incorrect* because of faulty grammar
  B. *Incorrect* because of faulty punctuation
  C. *Incorrect* because of faulty spelling
  D. *Correct*

Examine each sentence carefully. Then, print in the space at the right the letter preceding the category which is the BEST of the four suggested above
(Note: Each incorrect sentence contains only one type of error. Consider a sentence correct if it contains no errors, although there may be other correct ways of writing the sentence.)

1. Of the two employees, the one in our office is the most efficient.   1.____

2. No one can apply or even understand, the new rules and regulations.   2.____

3. A large amount of supplies were stored in the empty office.   3.____

4. If an employee is occassionally asked to work overtime, he should do so willingly.   4.____

5. It is true that the new procedures are difficult to use but, we are certain that you will learn them quickly.   5.____

6. The office manager said that he did not know who would be given a large allotment under the new plan.   6.____

7. It was at the supervisor's request that the clerk agreed to postpone his vacation.   7.____

8. We do not believe that it is necessary for both he and the clerk to attend the conference.   8.____

9. All employees, who display perseverance, will be given adequate recognition.   9.____

10. He regrets that some of us employees are dissatisfied with our new assignments.   10.____

11. "Do you think that the raise was merited," asked the supervisor?   11.____

12. The new manual of procedure is a valuable supplement to our rules and regulations.   12.____

13. The typist admitted that she had attempted to pursuade the other employees to assist her in her work.   13.____

2 (#5)

14. The supervisor asked that all amendments to the regulations be handled by 14.____
    you and I.

15. The custodian seen the boy who broke the window. 15.____

KEY (CORRECT ANSWERS)

1.	A	6.	D	11.	B
2.	B	7.	D	12.	C
3.	A	8.	A	13.	C
4.	C	9.	B	14.	A
5.	B	10.	D	15.	A

PREPARING WRITTEN MATERIALS

EXAMINATION SECTION
TEST 1

DIRECTIONS: Each of the two sentences in the following questions may contain errors in punctuation, capitalization, or grammar.
If there is an error in only Sentence I, mark your answer A. If there is an error in only Sentence II, mark your answer B.
If there is an error in both Sentence I and Sentence II, mark your answer C. If both Sentence I and II are correct, mark your answer D.
PRINT THE LETTER OF THE CORRECT ANSWER IN THE SPACE AT THE RIGHT.

1. I. The task of typing these reports is to be divided equally between you and me. 1.____
   II. If it was he, I would use a different method for filing these records.

2. I. The new clerk is just as capable as some of the older employees, if not more capable. 2.____
   II. Using his knowledge of arithmetic to check the calculation, the supervisor found no errors in the report.

3. I. A typist who does consistently superior work probably merits promotion. 3.____
   II. In its report on the stenographic unit, the committee pointed out that neither the stenographers nor the typists were adequately trained.

4. I. Entering the office, the desk was noticed immediately by the visitor. 4.____
   II. Arrangements have been made to give this training to whoever applies for it.

5. I. The office manager estimates that this assignment, which is to be handled by you and I, will require about two weeks for completion. 5.____
   II. One of the recommendations of the report is that these kind of forms be discarded because they are of no value.

6. I. The supervisor knew that the typist was a quiet, cooperative, efficient, employee. 6.____
   II. The duties of stenographer are to take dictation notes at conferences and transcribing them.

7. I. The stenographer has learned that she, as well as two typists, is being assigned to the new unit. 7.____
   II. We do not know who you have designated to take charge of the new program.

8. I. He asked, "When do you expect to return?" 8.____
   II. I doubt whether this system will be successful here; it is not suitable for the work of our agency.

9. I. It is a policy of this agency to encourage punctuality as a good habit for we employees to adopt.
   II. The successful completion of the task was due largely to them cooperating effectively with the supervisor.

10. I. Mr. Smith, who is a very competent executive has offered his services to our department.
    II. Every one of the stenographers who work in this office is considered trustworthy.

11. I. It is very annoying to have a pencil sharpener, which is not in proper working order.
    II. The building watchman checked the door of Charlie's office and found that the lock has been jammed.

12. I. Since he went on the New York City council a year ago, one of his primary concerns has been safety in the streets.
    II. After waiting in the doorway for about 15 minutes, a black sedan appeared.

13. I. When you are studying a good textbook is important.
    II. He said he would divide the money equally between you and me.

14. I. The question is, "How can a large number of envelopes be sealed rapidly without the use of sealing machine?"
    II. The administrator assigned two stenographers, Mary and I, to the new bureau.

15. I. A dictionary, in addition to the office management textbooks, were placed on his desk.
    II. The concensus of opinion is that none of the employees should be required to work overtime.

16. I. Mr. Granger has demonstrated that he is as courageous, if not more courageous, than Mr. Brown.
    II. The successful completion of the project depends on the manager's accepting our advisory opinion.

17. I. Mr. Ames was in favor of issuing a set of rules and regulations for all of us employees to follow.
    II. It is inconceivable that the new clerk knows how to deal with that kind of correspondence.

18. I. The revised refference manual is to be used by all of the employees.
    II. Mr. Johnson told Miss Kent and me to accumulate all the letters that we receive.

19. I. The supervisor said, that before any changes would be made in the attendance report, there must be ample justification for them.
    II. Each of them was asked to amend their preliminary report.

20. I. Mrs. Peters conferred with Mr. Roberts before she laid the papers on his desk.
    II. As far as this report is concerned, Mr. Williams always has and will be responsible for its preparation.

20.____

KEY (CORRECT ANSWERS)

1.	B	11.	C
2.	D	12.	C
3.	D	13.	A
4.	A	14.	B
5.	C	15.	C
6.	C	16.	A
7.	B	17.	B
8.	D	18.	A
9.	C	19.	C
10.	A	20.	B

TEST 2

DIRECTIONS: Each question or incomplete statement is followed by several suggested answers or completions. Select the one that BEST answers the question or completes the statement. *PRINT THE LETTER OF THE CORRECT ANSWER IN THE SPACE AT THE RIGHT.*

Questions 1-9.

DIRECTIONS: Questions 1 through 9 consist of pairs of sentences which may or may not contain errors in grammar, capitalization, or punctuation.
If both sentences are correct, mark your answer A.
If the first sentence only is correct, mark your answer B.
If the second sentence only is correct, mark your answer C.
If both sentences are incorrect, mark your answer D.
NOTE: Consider a sentence correct if it contains no errors, although there may be other correct ways of writing the sentence.

1. I. An unusual conference will be held today at George Washington high school. 1.____
    II. The principal of the school, Dr. Pace, described the meeting as "a unique opportunity for educators to exchange ideas.

2. I. Studio D, which they would ordinarily use, will be occupied at that time. 2.____
    II. Any other studio, which is properly equipped, may be used instead.

3. I. D.H. Lawrence's <u>Sons and Lovers</u> were discussed on today's program. 3.____
    II. Either Eliot's or Yeats's work is to be covered next week.

4. I. This program is on the air for three years now, and has a well-established audience. 4.____
    II. We have received many complimentary letters from listeners, and scarcely no critical ones.

5. I. Both Mr. Owen and Mr. Mitchell have addressed the group. 5.____
    II. As has Mr. Stone, whose talks have been especially well received.

6. I. The original program was different in several respects from the version that eventually went on the air. 6.____
    II. Each of the three announcers who Mr. Scott thought had had suitable experience was asked whether he would be willing to take on the special assignment.

7. I. A municipal broadcasting system provides extensive coverage of local events, but also reports national and international news. 7.____
    II. A detailed account of happenings in the South may be carried by a local station hundreds of miles away.

8. I. Jack Doe the announcer and I will be working on the program. 8.____
    II. The choice of musical selections has been left up to he and I.

148

9. I. Mr. Taylor assured us that "he did not anticipate any difficulty in making arrangements for the broadcast."
   II. Although there had seemed at first to be certain problems; these had been solved.

9._____

Questions 10-14.

DIRECTIONS: Questions 10 through 14 consist of pairs of sentences which may contain errors in grammar, sentence structure, punctuation, or spelling, or both sentences may be correct. Consider a sentence correct if it contains no errors, although there may be other correct ways of writing the sentence.
If only Sentence I contains an error, mark your answer A.
If only Sentence II contains an error, mark your answer B.
If both sentences contain errors, mark your answer C.
If both sentences are correct, mark your answer D.

10. I. No employee considered to be indispensable will be assigned to the new office.
    II. The arrangement of the desks and chairs give the office a neat appearance.

10._____

11. I. The recommendation, accompanied by a report, was delivered this morning.
    II. Mr. Green thought the procedure would facilitate his work; he knows better now.

11._____

12. I. Limiting the term "property" to tangible property, in the criminal mischief setting, accords with prior case law holding that only tangible property came within the purview of the offense of malicious mischief.
    II. Thus, a person who intentionally destroys the property of another, but under an honest belief that he has title to such property, cannot be convicted of criminal mischief under the Revised Penal Law.

12._____

13. I. Very early in its history, New York enacted statutes from time to time punishing, either as a felony or as a misdemeanor, malicious injuries to various kinds of property: piers, booms, dams, bridges, etc.
    II. The application of the statute is necessarily restricted to trespassory takings with larcenous intent: namely with intent permanently or virtually permanently to "appropriate" property or "deprive" the owner of its use.

13._____

14. I. Since the former Penal Law did not define the instruments of forgery in a general fashion, its crime of forgery was held to be narrower than the common law offense in this respect and to embrace only those instruments explicitly specified in the substantive provisions.
    II. After entering the barn through an open door for the purpose of stealing, it was closed by the defendants

14._____

Questions 15-20.

DIRECTIONS: Questions 15 through 20 consist of pairs of sentences which may or may not contain errors in grammar, capitalization, or punctuation.
If both sentences are correct, mark your answer A.
If the first sentence only is correct, mark your answer B.
If the second sentence only is correct, mark your answer C.
If both sentences are incorrect, mark your answer D.
NOTE: Consider a sentence correct if it contains no errors, although there may be other ways of writing the sentence.

15. I. The program, which is currently most popular, is a news broadcast.
    II. The engineer assured his supervisor that there was no question of his being late again.

16. I. The announcer recommended that the program originally scheduled for that time be cancelled.
    II. Copies of the script may be given to whoever is interested.

17. I. A few months ago it looked like we would be able to broadcast the concert live.
    II. The program manager, as well as the announcers, were enthusiastic about the plan.

18. I. No speaker on the subject of education is more interesting than he.
    II. If he would have had the time, we would have scheduled him for a regular weekly broadcast.

19. I. This quartet, in its increasingly complex variations on a simple theme, admirably illustrates Professor Baker's point.
    II. Listeners interested in these kind of ideas will find his recently published study of Haydn rewarding.

20. I. The Commissioner's resignation at the end of next month marks the end of a long public service career.
    II. Outstanding among his numerous achievements were his successful implementation of several revolutionary schemes to reorganize the agency.

KEY (CORRECT ANSWERS)

1.	C	11.	D
2.	B	12.	C
3.	C	13.	B
4.	D	14.	A
5.	B	15.	C
6.	A	16.	A
7.	A	17.	D
8.	D	18.	B
9.	D	19.	B
10.	B	20.	B

BASIC FUNDAMENTALS OF A FINANCIAL STATEMENT

TABLE OF CONTENTS

	PAGE
Commentary	1
Financial Reports	1
Balance Sheet	1
Assets	1
The ABC Manufacturing Co., Inc.	
Consolidated Balance Sheet – December 31	2
Fixed Assets	3
Depreciation	4
Intangibles	4
Liabilities	5
Reserves	6
Capital Stock	6
Surplus	6
What Does the Balance Sheet Show?	7
Net Working Capital	7
Inventory and Inventory Turnover	8
Net Book Value of Securities	8
Proportion of Bonds, Preferred and Common Stock	9
The Income Account	10
Cost of Sales	11
The ABC Manufacturing Co., Inc.	
Consolidated Income and Earned Surplus – December 31	11
Maintenance	12
Interest Charges	13
Net Income	13
Analyzing the Income Account	14
Interest Coverage	15
Earnings Per Common Share	15
Stock Prices	16
Important Terms and Concepts	17

BASIC FUNDAMENTALS OF A FINANCIAL STATEMENT

COMMENTARY

The ability to read and understand a financial statement is a basic requirement for the accountant, auditor, account clerk, bookkeeper, bank examiner, budget examiner, and, of course, for the executive who must manage and administer departmental affairs.

FINANCIAL REPORTS

Are financial reports really as difficult as all that? Well, if you know they are not so difficult because you have worked with them before, this section will be of auxiliary help for you. However, if you find financial statements a bit murky, but realize their great importance to you, we ought to get along fine together. For "mathematics," all we'll use is fourth-grade arithmetic.

Accountants, like all other professionals, have developed a specialized vocabulary. Sometimes this is helpful and sometimes plain confusing (like their practice of calling the income account, "Statement of Profit and Loss," when it is bound to be one or the other). But there are really only a score or so technical terms that you will have to get straight in mind. After that is done, the whole foggy business will begin to clear and in no time at all you'll be able to talk as wisely as the next fellow.

BALANCE SHEET

Look at the sample balance sheet printed on Page 2, and we'll have an insight into how it is put together. This particular report is neither the simplest that could be issued, nor the most complicated. It is a good average sample of the kind of report issues by an up-to-date manufacturing company.

Note particularly that the balance sheet represents the situation as it stood on one particular day, December 31, not the record of a year's operation. This balance sheet is broken into two parts on the left are shown *ASSETS* and on the right *LIABILITIES*. Under the asset column, you will find listed the value of things the company owns or are owed to the company. Under liabilities are listed the things the company owes to others, plus reserves, surplus, and the stated value of the stockholders' interest in the company.

One frequently hears the comment, "Well, I don't see what a good balance sheet is anyway, because the assets and liabilities are always the same whether the company is successful or not."

It is true that they always balance and, by itself, a balance sheet doesn't tell much until it is analyzed. Fortunately, we can make a balance sheet tell its story without too much effort—often an extremely revealing story, particularly, if we compare the records of several years.

ASSETS

The first notation on the asset side of the balance sheet is *CURRENT ASSETS* (Item 1). In general, current assets include cash and things that can be turned into cash in a hurry, or that, in the normal course of business, will be turned into cash in the reasonably near future, usually within a year.

Item 2 on our sample sheet is *CASH*. Cash is just what you would expect—bills and silver in the till and money on deposit in the bank.

UNITED STATES GOVERNMENT SECURITIES is Item 3. The general practice is to show securities listed as current assets at cost or market value, whichever is lower. The figure, for all reasonable purposes, represents the amount by which total cash could be easily increased if the company wanted to sell these securities.

The next entry is *ACCOUNTS RECEIVABLE* (Item 4). Here we find the total amount of money owed to the company by its regular business creditors and collectable within the next year. Most of the money is owed to the company by its customers for goods that the company delivered on credit. If this were a department store instead of a manufacturer, what you owed the store on our charge account would be included here. Because some people fail to pay their bills, the company sets up a reserve for doubtful accounts, which it subtracts from all the money owed.

THE ABC MANUFACTURING COMPANY, INC.
CONSOLIDATED BALANCE SHEET – DECEMBER 31

Item			Item		
1. CURRENT ASSETS			16. CURRENT LIABILITIES		
2. Cash			17. Accts. Payable		$300,000
3. U.S. Government Securities			18. Accrued Taxes		800,000
4. Accounts Receivable (less reserves)		2,000,000	19. Accrued Wages, interest and Other Expenses		370,000
5. Inventories (at lower of cost or market)		2,000,000	20. Total Current Liabilities		$1,470,000
6. Total Current Assets		$7,000,000	21. FIRST MORTGAGE SINKING FUND BONDS, 3½ % DUE 2020		$2,000,000
7. INVESTMENT IN AFFILIATED COMPANY Not consolidated (at cost, not in excess of net assets)		200,000	22. RESERVE FOR CONTINGENCIES		200,000
8. OTHER INVESTMENTS At cost, less than market		100,000	23. CAPITAL STOCK: 24. 5% Preferred Stock (authorized and issued		
9. PLANT IMPROVEMENT FUND		550,000	10,000 shares of $100 par shares of $100		
10. PROPERTY, PLANT AND EQUIPMENT: Cost	$8,000,000		(par value)	$1,000,000	
11. Less Reserve for Depreciation	5,000,000		25. Common stock (authorized and issued 400,000 shares of no		
12. NET PROPERTY		3,000,000	par value)	1,000,000	
13. PREPAYMENTS		50,000	26. SURPLUS:		2,000,000
14. DEFERRED CHARGES		100,000	27. Earned	3,530,000	
15. PATENTS AND GOODWILL		100,000	28. Capital (arising from sale of common capital stock at price in excess of stated value)	1,900,000	
					5,430,000
TOTAL		$11,000,000	TOTAL		$11,100,000

Item 5, *INVENTORIES*, is the value the company places on the supplies it owns. The inventory of a manufacturer may contain raw materials that it uses in making the things it sells, partially finished goods in process of manufacture, and, finally, completed merchandise that it is ready to sell. Several methods are used to arrive at the value placed on these various items. The most common is to value them at their cost or present market value, whichever is lower.

You can be reasonably confident, however, that the figure given is an honest and significant one for the particular industry if the report is certified by a reputable firm of public accountants.

Next on the asset side is *TOTAL CURRENT ASSETS* (Item 6). This is an extremely important figure when used in connection with other items in the report, which we will come to presently. Then we will discover how to make total current assets tell their story.

INVESTMENT IN AFFILIATED COMPANY Item 7) represents the cost to our parent company of the capital stock of its subsidiary or affiliated company. A subsidiary is simply one company that is controlled by another. Most corporations that own other companies outright lump the figures in a CONSOLIDATED BALANCE SHEET. This means that, under cash, for example, one would find a total figure that represented all of the cash of the parent company and of its wholly owned subsidiary. This is a perfectly reasonable procedure because, in the last analysis, all of the money is controlled by the same persons.

Our typical company shows that it has *OTHER INVESTMENTS* (Item 8), in addition to its affiliated company. Sometimes good marketable securities other than Government bonds are carried as current assets, but the more conservative practice is to list these other security holdings separately. If they have been bought as a permanent investment, they would always be shown by themselves. "At cost, less than market" means that our company paid $100,000 for these other investments, but they are now worth more.

Among our assets is a *PLANT IMPROVEMENT FUND* (Item 9). Of course, this item does not appear in all company balance sheets, but is typical of special funds that companies set up for one purpose or another. For example, money set aside to pay off part of the bonded debt of a company might be segregated into a special fund. The money our directors have put aside to improve the plant would often be invested in Government bonds,

FIXED ASSETS

The next item (10) is *PROPERTY, PLANT, AND EQUIPMENT*, but it might just as well be labeled Fixed Assets as these items are used more or less interchangeably, Under Item 10, the report gives the value of land, buildings, and machinery and such movable things as trucks, furniture, and hand tools. Historically, probably more sins were committed against this balance sheet item than any other.

In olden days, cattlemen used to drive their stock to market in the city. It was a common trick to stop outside of town, spread out some salt for the cattle to make them thirsty and then let them drink all the water they could hold. When they were weighed for sale, the cattlemen would collect cash for the water the stock had drunk. Business buccaneers, taking the cue from their farmer friends, would often "write up" the value of their fixed assets. In other words, they would increase the value shown on the balance sheet, making the capital stock appear to be worth a lot more than it was. *Watered stock* proved a bad investment for most stockholders. The practice has, fortunately, been stopped, though it took major financial reorganizations to squeeze the water out of some securities.

The most common practice today is to list fixed assets at cost. Often, there is no ready market for most of the things that fall under this heading, so it is not possible to give market value. A good report will tell what is included under fixed assets and how it has been valued. If the value has been increased by *write-up* or decreased by *write-down*, a footnote explanation is usually given. A *write-up* might occur, for instance, if the value of real estate increased substantially. A *write-down* might follow the invention of a new machine that put an important part of the company's equipment out of date.

DEPRECIATION

Naturally, all of the fixed property of a company will wear out in time (except, of course, non-agricultural land). In recognition of this fact, companies set up a *RESERVE FOR APPRECIATION* (Item 11). If a truck costs $4,000 and is expected to last four years, it will be depreciated at the rate of $1,000 a year.

Two other items also frequently occur in connection with depreciation—*depletion* and *obsolescence*. Companies may lump depreciation, depletion, and obsolescence under a single title, or list them separately.

Depletion is a term used primarily by mining and oil companies (or any of the so-called extractive industries). Depletion means exhaust or use up. As the oil or other natural resource is used up, a reserve is set up, to compensate for the natural wealth the company no longer owns. This reserve is set up in recognition of the fact that, as the company sells its natural product, it must get back not only the cost of extracting but also the original cost of the natural resource.

Obsolescence represents the loss in value because a piece of property has gone out of date before it wore out. Airplanes are modern examples of assets that tend to get behind the times long before the parts wear out. (Women and husbands will be familiar with the speed at which ladies' hats "obsolesce.")

In our sample balance sheet we have placed the reserve for depreciation under fixed assets and then subtracted, giving us *NET PROPERTY* (Item 12), which we add into the asset column. Sometimes, companies put the reserve for depreciation in the liability column. As you can see, the effect is just the same whether it is *subtracted* from assets or *added* to liabilities.

The manufacturer, whose balance sheet we use, rents a New York showroom and pays his rent yearly, in advance. Consequently, he has listed under assets *PREPAYMENTS* (Item 13). This is listed as an asset because he has paid for the use of the showroom, but has not yet received the benefit from its use. The use is something coming to the firm in the following year and, hence, is an asset. The dollar value of this asset will decrease by one-twelfth each month during the coming year.

DEFERRED CHARGES (Item 14) represents a type of expenditure similar to prepayment. For example, our manufacturer brought out a new product last year, spending $100,000 introducing it to the market. As the benefit from this expenditure will be returned over months or even years to come, the manufacturer did not think it reasonable to charge the full expenditure against costs during the year. He has *deferred* the charges and will write them off gradually.

INTANGIBLES

The last entry in our asset column is *PATENTS AND GOODWILL* (Item 15). If our company were a young one, set up to manufacturer some new patented product, it would probably carry its patents at a substantial figure. In fact, *intangibles* of both old and new companies are often of great but generally unmeasurable worth.

Company practice varies considerably in assigning value to intangibles. Proctor & Gamble, despite the tremendous goodwill that has been built up for *Ivory Soap*, has reduced all of its intangibles to the nominal $1. Some of the big cigarette companies, on the contrary, place a high dollar value on the goodwill their brand names enjoy. Companies that spend a good deal for research and the development of new products are more inclined than others to reflect this fact in the value assigned to patents, license agreements, etc.

LIABILITIES

The liability side of the balance sheet appears a little deceptive at first glance. Several of the entries simply don't sound like liabilities by any ordinary definition of the term.

The first term on the liability side of any balance sheet is usually CURRENT LIABILITIES (Item 16). This is a companion to the Current Assets item across the page and includes all debts that fall due within the next year. The relation between current assets and current liabilities is one of the most revealing things to be gotten from the balance sheet, but we will go into that quite thoroughly later on.

ACCOUNTS PAYABLE (Item 17) represents the money that the company owes to its ordinary business creditors—unpaid bills for materials, supplies, insurance, and the like. Many companies itemize the money they owe in a much more detailed fashion than we have done, but, as you will see, the totals are the most interesting thing to us.

Item 18, ACCRUED TAXES, is the tax bill that the company estimates it still owes for the past year. We have lumped all taxes in our balance sheet, as many companies do. However, sometimes you will find each type of tax given separately. If the detailed procedure is followed, the description of the tax is usually quite sufficient to identify the separate items.

Accounts Payable was defined as the money the company owed to its regular business creditors. The company also owes, on any given day, wages to its own employees; interest to its bondholders and to banks from which it may have borrowed money; fees to its attorneys; pensions, etc. These are all totaled under ACCRUED WAGES, INTEREST AND OTHER EXPENSES (Item 19).

TOTAL CURRENT LIABILITIES (Item 20) is just the sum of everything that the company owed on December 31 and which must be paid sometime in the next twelve months.

It is quite clear that all of the things discussed above are liabilities. The rest of the entries on the liability side of the balance sheet, however, do not seem at first glance to be liabilities.

Our balance sheet shows that the company, on December 31, had $2,000,000 of 3½ percent First Mortgage BONDS outstanding (Item 21). Legally, the money received by a company when it sells bonds is considered a loan to the company. Therefore, it is obvious that the company owes to the bondholders an amount equal to the face value or the *call price* of the bonds it has outstanding. The call price is a figure usually larger than the face value of the bonds at which price the company can *call* the bonds in from the bondholders and pay them off before they ordinarily fall due. The date that often occurs as part of the name of a bond is the date at which the company has promised to pay off the loan from the bondholders.

RESERVES

The next heading, RESERVE FOR CONTINGENCIES (Item 22) sounds more like an asset than a liability. "My reserves," you might say, "are dollars in the bank, and dollars in the bank are assets.

No one would deny that you have something there. In fact, the corporation treasurer also has his reserve for contingencies balanced by either cash or some kind of unspecified investment on the asset side of the ledger. His reason for setting up a reserve on the liability side of the balance sheet is a precaution against making his financial position seem better than it is. He decided that the company might have to pay out this money during the coming year if certain things happened. If he did not set up the "reserve," his surplus would appear larger by an amount equal to his reserve.

A very large reserve for contingencies or a sharp increase in this figure from the previous year should be examined closely by the investor. Often, in the past, companies tried to hide their true earnings by transferring funds into a contingency reserve. As a reserve looks somewhat like a true liability, stockholders were confused about the real value of their securities. When a reserve is not set up for protection against some very probable loss or expenditure, it should be considered by the investor as part of surplus.

CAPITAL STOCK

Below reserves there is a major heading, *CAPITAL STOCK* (Item 23). Companies may have one type of security outstanding, or they may have a dozen. All of the issues that represent shares of ownership are capital, regardless of what they are called on the balance sheet—preferred stock, preference stock, common stock, founders' shares, capital stock, or something else.

Our typical company has one issue of 5 percent *PREFERRED STOCK* (Item 24). It is called *preferred* because those who own it have a right to dividends and assets before the *common* stockholders—that is, the holders are in a preferred position as owners. Usually, preferred stockholders do not have a voice in company affairs unless the company fails to pay them dividends at the promised rate. Their rights to dividends are almost always *cumulative*. This simply means that all past dividends must be paid before the other stockholders can receive anything. Preferred stockholders are not creditors of the company so it cannot properly be said that the company *owes* them the value of their holdings. However, in case the company decided to go out of business, preferred stockholders would have a prior claim on anything that was left in the company treasury after all of the creditors, including the bondholders, were paid off. In practice, this right does not always mean much, but it does explain why the book value of their holdings is carried as a liability.

COMMON STOCK (Item 25) is simple enough as far as definition is concerned. It represents the rights of the ordinary owner of the company. Each company has as many owners as it has stockholders. The proportion of the company that each stockholder owns is determined by the number of shares he has. However, neither the book value of a no-par common stock, nor the par value of an issue that has a given par, can be considered as representing either the original sale price, the market value, or what would be left for the stockholders if the company were liquidated.

A profitable company will seldom be dissolved. Once things have taken such a turn that dissolution appears desirable, the stated value of the stock is generally nothing but a fiction. Even if the company is profitable as a going institution, once it ceases to function even its tangible assets drop in value because there is not usually a ready market for its inventory of raw materials and semi-finished goods, or its plant and machinery.

SURPLUS

The last major heading on the liability side of the balance sheet is *SURPLUS* (Item 26). The surplus, of course, is not a liability in the popular sense at all. It represents, on our balance sheet, the difference between the stated value of our common stock and the net assets behind the stock.

Two different kinds of surplus frequently appear on company balance sheets, and our company has both kinds. The first type listed is *EARNED* surplus (Item 27). Earned surplus is roughly similar to your own savings. To the corporation, earned surplus is that part of net income which has not been paid to stockholders as dividends. It still belongs to you, but the directors have decided that it is best for the company and the stockholders to keep it in the business. The surplus may be invested in the plant just as you might invest part of your savings in your home. It may also be in cash or securities.

In addition to the earned surplus, our company also has a CAPITAL surplus (Item 28) of $1,900.00, which the balance sheet explains arose from selling the stock at a higher cost per share than is given as its stated value. A little arithmetic shows that the stock is carried on the books at $2.50 a share while the capital surplus amounts to $4.75 a share. From this we know that the company actually received an average of $7.25 net a share for the stock when it was sold.

WHAT DOES THE BALANCE SHEET SHOW?

Before we undertake to analyze the balance sheet figures, a word on just what an investor can expect to learn is in order. A generation or more ago, before present accounting standards had gained wide acceptance, considerable imagination went into the preparation of balance sheets. This, naturally, made the public skeptical of financial reports. Today, there is no substantial ground for skepticism. The certified public accountant, the listing requirements of the national stock exchanges, and the regulations of the Securities and Exchange Commission have, for all practical purposes, removed the grounds for doubting the good faith of financial reports.

The investor, however, is still faced with the task of determining the significance of the figures. As we have already seen, a number of items are based, to a large degree, upon estimates, while others are, of necessity, somewhat arbitrary.

NET WORKING CAPITAL

There is one very important thing that we can find from the balance sheet and accept with the full confidence that we know what we are dealing with. That is net working capital, sometimes simply called working capital.

On the asset side of our balance sheet, we have added up all of the current assets and show the total as Item 6. On the liability side, Item 20 gives the total of current liabilities. *Net working capital* or *net current assets* is the difference left after subtracting current liabilities from current assets. If you consider yourself an investor rather than a speculator, you should always insist that any company in which you invest have a comfortable amount of working capital. The ability of a company to meet its obligations with ease, expand its volume as business expands and take advantage of opportunities as they present themselves, is, to an important degree, determined by its working capital.

Probably the question in your mind is: "*Just what does 'comfortable amount' of working capital mean?*" Well, there are several methods used by analysts to judge whether a particular company has a sound working capital position. The first rough test for an industrial company is to compare the working capital figure with the current liability total. Most analysts say that minimum safety requires that net working capital at least equal current liabilities. Or, put another way, current assets should be at least twice as large as current liabilities.

There are so many different kinds of companies, however, that this test requires a great deal of modification if it is to be really helpful in analyzing companies in different industries. To help you interpret the current position of a company in which you are considering investing, the *current ratio* is more helpful than the dollar total of working capital. The current ratio is current assets divided by current liabilities.

In addition to working capital and current ratio, there are two other ways of testing the adequacy of the current position. *Net quick assets* provide a rigorous and important test of a company's ability to meet its current obligations. Net quick assets are found by taking total current assets (Item 6) and subtracting the value of inventories (Item 5). A well-fixed industrial company should show a reasonable excess of quick assets over current liabilities.

Finally, many analysts say that a good industrial company should have at least as much working capital (current assets less current liabilities) as the total book value of its bonds and preferred stock. In other words, current liabilities, bonded debt, and preferred stock *altogether* should not exceed the current assets.

INVENTORY AND INVENTORY TURNOVER

In the recent past, there has been much talk of inventories. Many commentators have said that these carry a serious danger to company earnings if management allows them to increase too much. Of course, this has always been true, but present high prices have made everyone more inventory-conscious than usual.

There are several dangers in a large inventory position. In the first place, sharp drop in price may cause serious losses; also, a large inventory may indicate that the company has accumulated a big supply of unsalable merchandise. The question still remains, however: "What do we mean by large inventory?"

As you certainly realize, an inventory is large or small only in terms of the yearly turnover and the type of business. We can discover the annual turnover of our sample company by dividing inventories (Item 5) into total annual sales (item "a" on the income account).

It is also interesting to compare the value of the inventory of a company being studied with total current assets. Again, however, there is considerable variation between different types of companies, so that the relationship becomes significant only when compared with similar companies.

NET BOOK VALUE OF SECURITIES

There is one other very important thing that can be gotten from the balance sheet, and that is the net book or equity value of the company's securities. We can calculate the net book value of each of the three types of securities our company has outstanding by a little very simple arithmetic. *Book value* means *the value at which something is carried on the books of the company*.

The full rights of the bondholders come before any of the rights of the stockholders, so, to find the net book value or net tangible assets backing up the bonds we add together the balance sheet value of the bonds, preferred stock, common stock, reserve, and surplus. This gives us a total of $9,630,000, (We would not include contingency reserve if we were reasonably sure the contingency was going to arise, but, as general reserves are often equivalent to surplus, it is, usually, best to treat the reserve just as though it were surplus.) However, part of this value represents the goodwill and patents carried at $100,000, which is not a tangible item, so, to be conservative, we subtract this amount, leaving $9,530,000 as the total net book value of the bonds. This is equivalent to $4,765 for each $1,000 bond, a generous figure. To calculate the net book value of the preferred stock, we must eliminate the face value of the bonds, and then, following the same procedure, add the value of the preferred stock, common stock, reserve, and surplus, and subtract goodwill. This gives us a total net book value for the preferred stock of $7,530 or $753 for each share of $100 par value preferred. This is also very good coverage for the preferred stock, but we must examine current earnings before becoming too enthusiastic about the value of any security.

The net book value of the common stock, while an interesting figure, is not so important as the coverage on the senior securities. In case of liquidation, there is seldom much left for the common stockholders because of the normal loss in value of company assets when they are put up for sale, as mentioned before. The book value figure, however, does give us a basis for comparison with other companies. Comparisons of net book value over a period of years also show us if the company is a soundly growing one or, on the other hand, is losing ground. Earnings, however, are our important measure of common stock values, as we will see shortly.

The net book value of the common stock is found by adding the stated value of the common stock, reserves, and surplus and then subtracting patents and goodwill. This gives us a total net book value of $6,530,000. As there are 400,000 shares of common outstanding, each share has a net book value of $16.32. You must be careful not to be misled by book value figures, particularly of common stock. Profitable companies (Coca-Cola, for example) often show a very low net book value and very substantial earnings. Railroads, on the other hand, may show a high book value for their common stock but have such low or irregular earnings that the market price of the stock is much less than its apparent book value. Banks, insurance companies, and investment trusts are exceptions to what we have said about common stock net book value. As their assets are largely liquid (i.e., cash, accounts receivable, and marketable securities), the book value of their common stock sometimes indicates its value very accurately.

PROPORTION OF BONDS, PREFERRED AND COMMON STOCK

Before investing, you will want to know the proportion of each kind of security issued by the company you are considering. A high proportion of bonds reduces the attractiveness of both the preferred and common stock, while too large an amount of preferred detracts from the value of the common.

The *bond ratio* is found by dividing the face value of the bonds (Item 21), or $2,000,000, by the total value of the bonds, preferred stock, common stock, reserve, and surplus, or $9,630,000. This shows that bonds amount to about 20 percent of the total of bonds, capital, and surplus.

The *preferred stock ratio* is found in the same way, only we divide the stated value of the preferred stock by the total of the other five items. Since we have half as much preferred stock as we have bonds, the preferred ratio is roughly 10.

Naturally, the *common stock ratio* will be the difference between 100 percent and the totals of the bonds and preferred, or 70 percent in our sample company. You will want to remember that the most valuable method of determining the common stock ratio is in combination with reserve and surplus. The surplus, as we have noted, is additional backing for the common stock and usually represents either original funds paid in to the company in excess of the stated value of the common stock (capital surplus), or undistributed earnings (earned surplus).

Most investment analysts carefully examine industrial companies that have more than about a quarter of their capitalization represented by bonds, while common stock should total at least as much as all senior securities (bonds and preferred issues). When this is not the case, companies often find it difficult to raise new capital. Banks don't like to lend them money because of the already large debt, and it is sometimes difficult to sell common stock because of all the bond interest or preferred dividends that must be paid before anything is available for the common stockholder.

Railroads and public utility companies are exceptions to most of the rules of thumb that we use in discussing The ABC Manufacturing Company, Inc. Their situation is different because of the tremendous amounts of money they have invested in their fixed assets, their small inventories and he ease with which they can collect their receivables. Senior securities of railroads and utility companies frequently amount to more than half of their capitalization, Speculators often interest themselves in companies that have a high proportion of debt or preferred stock because of the *leverage factor*. A simple illustration will show why. Let us take, for example, a company with $10,000,000 of 4 percent bonds outstanding. If the company is earning $440,000 before bond interest, there will be only $40,000 left for the common stock ($10,000,000 at 4% equals $400,000). However, an increase of only 10 percent in earnings (to $484,000) will leave $84,000 for common stock dividends, or an increase of more than 100 percent. If there is only a small common issue, the increase in earnings per share would appear very impressive.

You have probably already noticed that a decline of 10 percent in earnings would not only wipe out everything available for the common stock, but result in the company being unable to cover its full interest on its bonds without dipping into surplus. This is the great danger of so-called high leverage stocks and also illustrates the fundamental weakness of companies that have a disproportionate amount of debt or preferred stock. Investors would do well to steer clear of them. Speculators, however, will continue to be fascinated by the market opportunities they offer.

THE INCOME ACCOUNT

The fundamental soundness of a company, as shown by its balance sheet, is important to investors, but of even greater interest is the record of its operation. Its financial structure shows much of its ability to weather storms and pick up speed when times are good. It is the income record, however, that shows us how a company is actually doing and gives us our best guide to the future.

The *Consolidated Income and Earned Surplus* account of our company is stated on the next page. Follow the items given there and we will find out just how our company earned its money, what it did with its earnings, and what it all means in terms of our three classes of securities. We have used a combined income and surplus account because it is the form most frequently followed by industrial companies. However, sometimes the two statements are given separately. Also, a variety of names are used to describe this same part of the financial report. Sometimes it is called profit and loss account, sometimes *record of earnings*, and, often, simply *income account*. They are all the same thing.

The details that you will find on different income statements also vary a great deal. Some companies show only eight or ten separate items, while others will give a page or more of closely spaced entries that break down each individual type of revenue or cost. We have tried to strike a balance between extremes; give the major items that are in most income statements, omitting details that are only interesting to the expert analyst.

The most important source of revenue always makes up the first item on the income statement. In our company, it is *Net Sales* (Item "a"). If it were a railroad or a utility instead of a manufacturer, this item would be called *gross revenues*. In any case, it represents the money paid into the company by its customers. Net sales are given to show that the figure represents the amount of money actually received after allowing for discounts and returned goods.

Net sales or gross revenues, you will note, is given before any kind of miscellaneous revenue that might have been received from investments, the sale of company property, tax refunds, or the like. A well-prepared income statement is always set up this way so that the stockholder can estimate the success of the company in fulfilling its major job of selling goods or service. If this were not so, you could not tell whether the company was really losing or making money on its operations, particularly over the last few years when tax rebates and other unusual things have often had great influence on final net income figures.

The ABC Manufacturing Company, Inc.
CONSOLIDATED INCOME AND EARNED SURPLUS
For the Year Ended December 31

Item		
a. Sales		$10,000,000
b. COST OF SALES, EXPENSES AND OTHER OPERATING CHARGES:		
c. Cost of Goods Sold	$7,000,000	
d. Selling, Administrative & Gen. Expenses	500,000	
e. Depreciation	200,000	
f. Maintenance and Repairs	400,000	
g. Taxes (Other than Federal Inc. Taxes)	300,000	8,400,000
h. NET PROFIT FROM OPERATIONS		$1,600,000
i. OTHER INCOME:		
j. Royalties and Dividends	$250,000	
k. Interest	25,000	
l. TOTAL		$1,875,000
m. INTEREST CHARGES:		
n. Interest on Funded Debt	$70,000	
o. Other Interest	20,000	90,000
p. NET INCOME BEFORE PROVISION FOR FED. INCOME TAXES		$1,785,000
q. PROVISION FOR FEDERAL INCOME TAXES		678,300
r. NET INCOME		$1,106,700
s. DIVIDENDS		
t. Preferred Stock - $5.00 Per Share	$50,000	
u. Common Stock - $1.00 Per Share	400,000	
v. PROVISION FOR CONTINGENCIES	200,000	650,000
w. BALANCE CARRIED TO EARNED SURPLUS		456,700
x, EARNED SURPLUS – JANUARY 1		3,073,000
y. EARNED SURPLUS – DECEMBER 31		$3,530,000

COST OF SALES

A general heading, *Cost of Sales, Expenses, and Other Operating Charges* (Item "b") is characteristic of a manufacturing company, but a utility company or railroad would call all of these things *operating expenses*.

The most important subdivision is *Cost of Goods Sold* (Item "c"). Included under cost of goods sold are all of the expenses that go directly into the manufacture of the products the company sells—raw materials, wages, freight, power, and rent. We have lumped these expenses together, as many companies do. Sometimes, however, you will find each item listed separately. Analyzing a detailed income account is a pretty technical operation and had best be left to the expert.

We have shown separately, opposite "d," the *Selling, Administrative and General Expenses* of the past year. Unfortunately, there is little uniformity among companies in their treatment of these important non-manufacturing costs. Our figure includes the expenses of management; that is, executive salaries and clerical costs; commissions and salaries paid to salesmen; advertising expenses, and the like.

Depreciation ("e") shows us the amount that the company transferred from income during the year to the depreciation reserve that we ran across before as Item "11" on the balance sheet (Page 2). Depreciation must be charged against income unless the company is going to live on its own fat, something that no company can do for long and stay out of bankruptcy.

MAINTENANCE

Maintenance and Repairs (Item "f") represents the money spent to keep the plant in good operating order. For example, the truck that we mentioned under depreciation must be kept running day by day. The cost of new tires, recharging the battery, painting and mechanical repairs are all maintenance costs. Despite this day-to-day work on the truck, the company must still provide for the time when it wears out—hence, the reserve for depreciation.

You can readily understand from your own experience the close connection between maintenance and depreciation. If you do not take good care of your own car, you will have to buy a new one sooner than you would had you maintained it well. Corporations face the same problem with all of their equipment. If they do not do a good job of maintenance, much more will have to be set aside for depreciation to replace the abused tools and property.

Taxes are always with us. A profitable company always pays at least two types of taxes. One group of taxes are paid without regard to profits, and include real estate taxes, excise taxes, social security, and the like (Item "g"). As these payments are a direct part of the cost of doing business, they must be included before we can determine the *Net Profit From Operations* (Item "h").

Net Profit From Operations (sometimes called *gross profit*) tells us what the company made from manufacturing and selling its products. It is an interesting figure to investors because it indicates how efficiently and successfully the company operates in its primary purpose as a creator of wealth. As a glance at the income account will tell you, there are still several other items to be deducted before the stockholder can hope to get anything. You can also easily imagine that for many companies these other items may spell the difference between profit and loss. For these reasons, we use net profit from operations as an indicator of progress in manufacturing and merchandising efficiency, not as a judge of the investment quality of securities.

Miscellaneous Income not connected with the major purpose of the company is generally listed after net profit from operations. There are quite a number of ways that corporations increase their income, including interest and dividends on securities they own, fees for special services performed, royalties on patents they allow others to use, and tax refunds. Our income statement shows *Other Income* as Item "i," under which is shown income from *Royalties* and *Dividends* (Item "j"), and as a separate entry, *Interest* (Item "k") which the company received from its bond investments. The *Total* of other income (Item "l") shows us how much The ABC Manufacturing Company received from so-called *outside activities*. Corporations with diversified interests often receive tremendous amounts of other income.

INTEREST CHARGES

There is one other class of expenses that must be deducted from our income before we can determine the base on which taxes are paid, and that is *Interest Charges* (Item "m"). As our company has $2,000,000 worth of 3 ½ percent bonds outstanding, it will pay *Interest* on Funded Debt of $70,000 (Item "n"). During the year, the company also borrowed money from the bank, on which it, of course, paid interest, shown as *Other Interest* (Item "o").

Net Income Before Provision for Federal Income Taxes ("Item "p") is an interesting figure for historical comparison. It shows us how profitable the company was in all of its various operations. A comparison of this entry over a period of years will enable you to see how well the company had been doing as a business institution before the government stepped in for its share of net earnings. Federal taxes have varied so much in recent years that earnings before taxes are often a real help in judging business progress.

A few paragraphs back we mentioned that a profitable corporation pays two general types of taxes. We have already discussed those that are paid without reference to profits. *Provision for Federal Income Taxes* (Item "q") is ordinarily figured on the total income of the company after normal business expenses, and so appears on our income account below these charges. Bond interest, for example, as it is payment on a loan, is deducted beforehand. Preferred and common stock dividends, which are profits that go to owners of the company, come after all charges and taxes.

NET INCOME

After we have deducted all of our expenses and income taxes from total income, we get *Net Income* (Item "r"). Net income is the most interesting figure of all to the investor. Net income is the amount available to pay dividends on the preferred and common stock. From the balance sheet, we have learned a good deal about the company's stability and soundness of structure; from net profit from operations, we judge whether the company is improving in industrial efficiency. Net income tells us whether the securities of the company are likely to be a profitable investment.

The figure given for a single year is not nearly all of the store, however. As we have noted before, the historical record is usually more important than the figure for any given year. This is just as true of net income as any other item. So many things change from year to year that care must be taken not to draw hasty conclusions. During the war, Excess Profits Taxes had a tremendous effect on the earnings of many companies. In the next few years, carryback tax credits allowed some companies to show a net profit despite the fact that they had operated at a loss. Even net income can be a misleading figure unless one examines it carefully. A rough and easy way of judging how sound a figure it is would be to compare it with previous years.

The investor in stocks has a vital interest in *Dividends* (Item "s"). The first dividend that our company must pay is that on its *Preferred Stock* (Item "t"). Some companies will even pay preferred dividends out of earned surplus accumulated in the past if the net income is not large enough, but such a company is skating on thin ice unless the situation is most unusual.

The directors of our company decided to pay dividends totaling ($400,000 on the *Common Stock*, or $1 a share (Item "u"). As we have noted before, the amount of dividends paid is not determined by net income, but by a decision of the stockholders' representatives—the company's directors. Common dividends, just like preferred dividends, can be paid out of surplus if there is little or no net income. Sometimes companies do this if they have a long history of regular payments and don't want to spoil the record because of some special temporary situation that caused them to lose money. This occurs even less frequently and is more dangerous than paying preferred dividends out of surplus.

It is much more common, on the contrary, to plough earnings back into the business—a phrase you frequently see on the financial pages and in company reports. The directors of our typical company have decided to pay only $1 on the common stock, though net income would have permitted them to pay much more. They decided that the company should save the difference.

The next entry on our income account, *Provision for Contingencies* (Item "v") shows us where our reserve for contingencies arose. The treasurer of our typical company has put the provision for contingencies after dividends. However, you will discover, if you look at very many financial reports, that it is sometimes placed above net income.

All of the net income that was not paid out as dividends, or set aside for contingencies, is shown as *Balance Carried to Earned Surplus* (Item "w"). In other words, it is kept in the business. In previous years, the company had also earned more than it paid out so it had already accumulated by the beginning of the year an earned surplus of $3,073,000 (Item "x"). When we total the earned surplus accumulated during the year to that which the company had at the first of the year, we get the total earned surplus at the end of the year (Item "y"). You will notice that the total here is the same as that which we ran across on the balance sheet as Item 27.

Not all companies combine their income and surplus account. When they do not, you will find that *balance carried to surplus* will be the last item on the income account. The statement of consolidated surplus would appear as a third section of the corporation's financial report. A separate surplus account might be used if the company shifted funds for reserves to surplus during the year or made any other major changes in its method of treating the surplus account.

ANALYZING THE INCOME ACCOUNT

The income account, like the balance sheet, will tell us a lot more if we make a few detailed comparisons. The size of the totals on an income account doesn't mean much by itself. A company can have hundreds of millions of dollars in net sales and be a very bad investment. On the other hand, even a very modest profit in round figure may make a security attractive if there are only a small number of shares outstanding.

Before you select a company for investment, you will want to know something of its *margin of profit*, and how this figure has changed over the years. Finding the margin of profit is very simple. We just divide the net profit from operations (Item "h") by net sales (Item "a"). The figure we get (0.16) shows us that the company made a profit of 16 percent from operations. By itself, though, this is not very helpful. We can make it significant in two ways.

In the first place, we can compare it with the margin of profit in previous years, and, from this comparison, learn if the company excels other companies that do a similar type of business. If the margin of profit of our company is very low in comparison with other companies in the same field, it is an unhealthy sign. Naturally, if it is high, we have grounds to be optimistic.

Analysts also frequently use *operating ratio* for the same purpose. The operating ratio is the complement of the margin of profit. The margin of profit of our typical company is 16. The operating ratio is 84. You can find the operating ratio either by subtracting the margin of profit from 100 or dividing the total of operating costs ($8,400,000) by net sales ($10,000,000).

The margin of profit figure and the operating ratio, like all of those ratios we examined in connection with the balance sheet, give us general information about the company, help us judge its prospects for the future. All of these comparisons have significance for the long term as they tell us about the fundamental economic condition of the company. But you still have the right to ask: "Are the securities good investments for me now?"

Investors, as opposed to speculators, are primarily interested in two things. The first is safety for their capital and the second, regularity of income. They are also interested in the rate of return on their investment but, as you will see, the rate of return will be affected by the importance placed on safety and regularity. High income implies risk. Safety must be bought by accepting a lower return.

The safety of any security is determined primarily by the earnings of the company that are available to pay interest or dividends on the particular issues. Again, though, round dollar figures aren't of much help to us. What we want to know is the relationship between the total money available and the requirements for each of the securities issued by the company.

INTEREST COVERAGE

As the bonds of our company represent part of its debt, the first thing we want to know is how easily the company can pay the interest. From the income account we see that the company had total income of $1,875,000 (Item "1"). The interest charge on our bonds each year is $70,000 (3½ percent of $2,000,000—Item 21 on the balance sheet). Dividing total income by bond interest charges ($1,875,000 by $70,000) shows us that the company earned its bond interest 26 times over. Even after income taxes, bond interest was earned 17 times, a method of testing employed by conservative analysts. Before an industrial bond should be considered a safe investment, so our company has a wide margin of safety.

To calculate the *preferred dividend coverage* (i.e., the number of times preferred dividends were earned), we must use net income as our base, as Federal Income Taxes and all interest charges must be paid before anything is available for stockholders. As we have 10,000 shares of $100 par value of preferred stock which pays a dividend of 5 percent, the total dividend requirement for the preferred stock is $50,000 (Items 24 on the balance sheet and "t" on the income account).

EARNINGS PER COMMON SHARE

The buyer of common stocks is often more concerned with the earnings per share of his stock than he is with the dividend. It is usually earnings per share or, rather, prospective earnings per share, that influence stock market prices. Our income account does not show the earnings available for the common stock, so we must calculate it ourselves. It is net income less preferred dividends (Items "r"- "t"), or $1,056,700. From the balance sheet, we know that there are 400,000 shares outstanding, so the company earned about $2.64 per share.

All of these ratios have been calculated for a single year. It cannot be emphasized too strongly, however, that the record is more important to the investor than the report of any single year. By all the tests we have employed, both the bonds and the preferred stock of our typical company appear to be very good investments, if their market prices were not too high. The investor would want to look back, however, to determine whether the operations were reasonably typical of the company.

Bonds and preferred stocks that are very safe usually sell at pretty high prices, so the yield to the investor is small. For example, if our company has been showing about the same coverage on its preferred dividends for many years and there is good reason to believe that the future will be equally kind, the company would probably replace the old 5 percent preferred with a new issue paying a lower rate, perhaps 4 percent.

16

STOCK PRICES

As the common stock does not receive a guaranteed dividend, its market value is determined by a great variety of influences in addition to the present yield of the stock measured by its dividends. The stock market, by bringing together buyers and sellers from all over the world, reflects their composite judgment of the present and future value of the stock. We cannot attempt here to write a treatise on the stock market. There is one important ratio, however, that every common stock buyer considers. That is the ratio of earnings to market price.

The so-called *price-earnings ratio* is simply the earnings per share on the common stock divided into the market price. Our typical company earned $2.64 a common share in the year. If the stock were selling at $30 a share, its price-earnings ratio would be about 11.4. This is the basis figure that you would want to use in comparing the common stock of this particular company with other similar stocks.

17
IMPORTANT TERMS AND CONCEPTS

LIABILITIES
WHAT THE COMPANY OWES—+ RESERVES + SURPLUS + STOCKHOLDERS INTEREST IN THE COMPANY

ASSETS
WHAT THE COMPANY OWNS— + WHAT IS OWED TO THE COMPANY

FIXED ASSETS
MACHINERY, EQUIPMENT, BUILDINGS, ETC.

EXAMPLES OF FIXED ASSETS
DESKS, TABLES, FILING CABINETS, BUILDINGS, LAND, TIMBERLAND, CARS AND TRUCKS, LOCOMOTIVES AND FREIGHT CARS, SHIPYARDS, OIL LANDS, ORE DEPOSITS, FOUNDRIES

EXAMPLES OF:

PREPAID EXPENSES
PREPAID INSURANCE, PREPAID RENT, PREPAIDD ROYALTIES AND PREPAID INTEREST

DEFERRED CHARGES
AMORTIZATION OF BOND DISCOUNT, ORGANIZATION EXPENSE, MOVING EXPENSES, DEVELOPMENT EXPENSES

ACCOUNTS PAYABLE
BILLS THE COMPANY OWES TO OTHERS

BONDHOLDERS ARE CREDITORS
BOND CERTIFICATES ARE IOU'S ISSUED BY A COMPANY BACKED BY A PLEDGE

BONDHOLDERS ARE OWNERS
A STOCK CERTIFICATE IS EVIDENCE OF THE SHAREHOLDER'S OWNERSHIP

EARNED SURPLUS
INCOME PLOWED BACK INTO THE BUSINESS

NET SALES
GROSS SALES MINUS DISCOUNTS AND RETURNED GOODS

NET INCOME
= TOTAL INCOME MINUS ALL EXPENSES AND INCOME TAXES